The Website Investor

The Website Investor

The Guide to Buying an Online Website Business for Passive Income

Jeff Hunt

NEW YORK

The Website Investor
The Guide to Buying an Online Website Business for Passive Income

© 2015 **Jeff Hunt**.

Published in New York, New York, by Morgan James Publishing. Morgan James and The Entrepreneurial Publisher are trademarks of Morgan James, LLC. www.MorganJamesPublishing.com

The Morgan James Speakers Group can bring authors to your live event. For more information or to book an event visit The Morgan James Speakers Group at www.TheMorganJamesSpeakersGroup.com.

A **free** eBook edition is available with the purchase of this print book.

CLEARLY PRINT YOUR NAME ABOVE IN UPPER CASE

Instructions to claim your free eBook edition:
1. Download the BitLit app for Android or iOS
2. Write your name in **UPPER CASE** on the line
3. Use the BitLit app to submit a photo
4. Download your eBook to any device

ISBN 978-1-63047-366-2 paperback
ISBN 978-1-63047-368-6 eBook
ISBN 978-1-63047-367-9 hardcover
Library of Congress Control Number:
2014946051

Cover Design by:
Chris Treccani
www.3dogdesign.net

Interior Design by:
Bonnie Bushman
bonnie@caboodlegraphics.com

In an effort to support local communities, raise awareness and funds, Morgan James Publishing donates a percentage of all book sales for the life of each book to Habitat for Humanity Peninsula and Greater Williamsburg.

Get involved today, visit
www.MorganJamesBuilds.com

Habitat for Humanity®
Peninsula and
Greater Williamsburg
Building Partner

To Becky,
my best investment

Contents

How You Can Be a Shark in the Online Business Tank

Have you ever wanted to own your own business?

Do you want the flexibility of working for yourself without all the headaches that come along with typical, physical businesses?

Are you looking for a place to put your money to get fantastic returns?

You've picked up the right book. In this short volume, you will learn how websites generate consistent monthly income that can supplement or replace your job.

You'll learn how you can buy and operate a website that is already earning cash and not have to build anything from scratch.

Many websites are real businesses with customers, products and monthly earnings but they don't cost hundreds of thousands of dollars to acquire. The strategies in these pages can make you the venture capitalist shark even if cash is in short supply.

I have learned the tips and techniques you see here through years of personal trial and error. I make my living through website investment. You can too.

Get ready to claim your share of the world's hottest digital real estate. The Where, the What and the How are all right here. All you need is the "Will" to join the ranks of successful website investors.

Introduction: You're Busted– Face the Camera

The seller was almost giddy as he described how his website grew by thousands of pages every day without him having to do a blessed thing. I couldn't see him because we were on the phone, but I could swear he was waving his arms because it sounded like he was bumping into things as he talked with his hands.

"Google loves this site, just L-U-V-S it," he said with exuberance. Half an hour later, I had sent him enough money to buy a used Honda Civic, and he turned over the keys of his beloved website. I was in the mugshot business.

"What the heck is the mugshot business?" my wife asked. Oops, I should have run this one by her first. It was too late now.

"This guy Brian made these genius little programs that collect mugshot photos and arrest information from jails all over Utah," I explained. "Then he puts them on his website for all the world to see. Oh, and it's all automatic."

"Why would anyone want to look at a mugshot?" She scrunched up her face.

"I have no idea, but 30,000 people dropped in last month." And there would soon be many more viewers than that.

Another question my wife posed: "Aren't the criminals gonna be unhappy about you plastering their pictures everywhere?"

"Uh, yeah, I asked him about that, and he said I might get some flame mail, but I could just take down the pictures of the whiners. Besides, we're a long way from Utah," I said, not sounding all that confident.

Brian was right. After thirty days, traffic to the site was way up. Earnings had increased by 66%. I was starting to feel pretty darn giddy myself.

However, there was one big problem. Brian had told me that the programmer who wrote the nifty software to find and publish arrest records had started to make impossible demands. While Brian had taken care of him, I was stuck without a programmer, trying to figure out how the system worked and how to scale everything up. A solution soon presented itself, and in a week or two, I was able to collect mugshots myself from any jail website that published arrest information.

It was all perfectly legal. Arrest information published by local law enforcement agencies is considered public record, and its re-publication is protected by federal law. So why did I hesitate to tell people about the newest addition to my website portfolio? Never mind that. This thing had potential, and I was going to run with it.

Utah was doing great, so I decided that it was time to branch out. Florida has a huge population, lots of big cities, and jail websites filled with pictures, so I started there. I also picked Oklahoma. I don't know why; I guess I'm just partial to Oklahoma.

Three weeks later, the Florida and Oklahoma sites were already getting hits and making a modest amount of revenue. I had never seen new websites get on their feet so fast. Meanwhile, Utah was still growing by leaps and bounds. The iron was hot, and now was the time to strike.

It was summer, and the kids were fidgeting without a lot to do. I walked into the family room and announced that I was going to teach everyone a new trick called "jail research." I had already prepared a list of states, and the family's job was to do Google searches within assigned states, looking for cities and sheriff offices with the most daily arrests. They were to record all their findings and report back with a list of jails that had information that looked easy to harvest. My wife, seventeen-year-old son, sixteen-year-old daughter, and twelve-year-old son each sat at his or her laptop or computer. The job was done in an afternoon.

Then the real fun began. Using the experience from Utah, Florida, and Oklahoma, the family room became command central, and everybody learned how to clone a mugshot website of his or her very own. Each person was assigned a state. Step by step, we walked through purchasing a domain name, installing Wordpress, doing designs and logos, setting up the locations and categories, and putting money-earning ads on each site. While the fam was working on the websites, I started getting all the jails set up to send us records.

Two and a half months after buying the Utah site, revenue had doubled, and traffic had tripled. We now had a total of ten websites. Most of the volume was still coming from the original Utah site, but some of the other states were growing quickly and becoming important contributors. In my home, sibling rivalry took a new form. The kids were each cheering for his or her own state, with Arizona and Georgia most often in the lead.

The family mugshot business was thriving, but we started to hear from folks whose pictures appeared on the website. We only received a few unhappy emails each month, which is surprising given the thousands of new mugshots that went up every day. However, the mail we did receive was rather intense. Some were indignant and threatening. Others were just matter of fact. One dad said he got a DUI and was worried about his young son Googling his name and seeing his mugshot come up. Another girl was scared to death that she would lose her job if her employer saw what she had done. In each case, we took down the picture and wondered whether this whole venture was such a good idea after all.

Along with posting shots, we also offered to send physical letters to inmates. A site visitor could pay us two dollars, give us the name of the inmate, and type in a message. We printed it out and put it in the mail. Senders could purchase upgrades like special paper, colored envelopes, a printed picture, whiff of perfume, or smiley and heart stickers. I can't reproduce any of the letters here because of confidentiality, but there were some tear-jerkers. One began, "You don't know me, but I'm your son…" Another, "I just had to pick out the ring by myself…" One letter included quite a shocker: "We shot him as he came out of the trees…" After having a near heart attack, I was revived when it became clear the writer was talking about a deer.

As we entered the fifth month, traffic across all the sites reached over 11,000 page views per day, which was a growth factor of 11x from when we started. Revenue had grown to over $6,000 per month—10x more than Utah was earning when we purchased it.

I bought the site because of its earning potential, and it didn't disappoint. Eventually, we decided to sell as it became increasingly difficult to justify earning money from posting photos that people didn't want published. The site sold for $30,000, and we netted a total of $49,000, start to finish, over five months. And I slept better at night.

It is exhilarating when an investment takes off. But where do you find these nuggets? And how do you make sure you are mining for gold and not plucking lemons? Read on my friend. Success is for the prepared, not the naïve.

1. Why Buy Websites?

I love investing in websites, and I love it for many reasons. Much of the income can be passive. The time investment is very flexible, and I get to learn about all kinds of subject areas, from dog breeding to magic shows. I don't have a boss. I avoid the commute to work, and I don't have to deal with customers or employees. I have the stereotypical work-at-home, sit-on-the-porch-with-my-laptop job and lifestyle. What's not to love about that?

> The biggest reason to invest in websites is the fantastic financial returns.

Even with all these fabulous perks to enjoy, the biggest reason I love investing in websites is the fantastic financial returns. Websites can deliver double-digit returns on investment every single month. You'll see a case study at the end of this chapter about a healthcare website. My initial investment was only $10,000, yet I gain $600 to $700 back from that website every month. That is a 70-80% annual return on my money. It is very difficult to find that kind of return in any other kind of investment strategy. Is it risky? Of course there are risks, but that's a different chapter.

So how much can you make with websites? Clearly, like everything else, the more you spend, the more you can make. But also, like other kinds of business investments, if you are willing to put a little bit of effort in along with your money, you can make a little more. And, if you are willing to put in a lot of effort, you can make a lot of money.

"Anyone who is not investing now is missing a tremendous opportunity."

–Carlos Slim

Is Website Investing Truly Passive?

As I said, one reason I love website investments is because there is the potential to have a passive income stream. There are some kinds of websites, like the healthcare website I mentioned, that are content websites. You put good information on the pages, and people visit to read the information. You make money when the visitors click on ads or when the advertisers pay you.

Other websites require more activity on your part. For example, eCommerce websites require you to buy products and ship them when customers order from you. So there is a wide range of effort when it comes to the level of passivity involved in owning a website. There is also a broad spectrum of people who are interested in this exciting kind of investment. Some don't want to spend any time at all working on their websites; others are willing to invest a little time in order to increase earnings. Still others, sensing the potential for huge returns, are willing to expend a great deal of effort to have a shot at substantial profits.

Traditional Businesses vs. Websites

Websites have greater returns than traditional businesses because they have lower overhead costs. With no buildings to buy, no fixtures or equipment to install, and no trucks to lease, the startup costs are minimal. Likewise, the ongoing costs are minimal. Because many of the products are digital or service-oriented, there is limited cost invested in goods sold.

"The difference between a successful person and others is not a lack of strength, not a lack of knowledge, but rather a lack in will."

–Vince Lombardi

Businesses have traditionally had physical and intangible assets. Websites have a third category of assets: digital assets. They are tangible because you can actually see them. You can go to a website and download the eBook or look at the pictures and read the articles. However, they are not physical, and they do not have the same level of cost as physical assets. As a result, once a digital asset is created, it can be sold at near 100% profit on an ongoing basis. So the nature of website business assets makes it possible for websites to have a much higher return on assets and return on your investment than traditional businesses.

While this characteristic of website businesses allows for much greater rewards, it also leaves the door open for greater risk. Digital assets do not have their value in physical material or function. They cannot always be repurposed like a building, land, or a vehicle. So their value is dictated by what customers are willing pay—regardless of how much it cost to create the asset to begin with.

The life cycle of a website tends to be shorter than that of a physical-asset-based business.

As a result, the value of a website can grow very quickly—and go away just as quickly. Does this mean that website investing is inherently risky? Not necessarily. It is certainly no more risky to buy a website than to buy a traditional business, or to buy stock for that matter. However, the life cycle of a website tends to be shorter than that of a physical-asset-based business.

Case Study: Healthy Business

Some would call my wish list for the perfect website purchase a pipe dream. I wanted a low-effort or "no-effort" site. It needed to be low risk and have better than average longevity. I was looking for something that was not dependent on whimsical changes made by Google. Preferably, it would have a payback period of twelve to fifteen months. It would also provide a useful service or quality product for its customers.

A health information website caught my eye. It was fifteen years old and still operated by the woman who had created it. She had worked as a patient educator her whole career and was ready to retire. The website was a labor of love for her. The articles on the site were a product of extensive interviews with nurses and physicians, as well as a repository of her experiences in healthcare. The owner wrote all the content herself, and she worked hard to ensure a non-academic, user friendly style that was both easy to read and thorough.

The owner was also something of a SEO (Search Engine Optimization) expert and had tweaked her titles, text, and interlinking structure to maximize keyword ranking in the search engines. Her attention to those details paid off as traffic during the month of the website auction was over 170,000 unique visitors. She had not participated in any of the "black-hat," ill-conceived schemes for fooling search engines to send traffic to the site. Specifically, she had never purchased backlinks. As a result, each time Google tightened the standards by changing the website ranking algorithms, the site's rankings had improved.

"Always bear in mind that your own resolution to succeed is more important than any one thing."

—Abraham Lincoln

The risk in this investment was the lack of earnings. There was a good reason for that. She hadn't put any energy into making a profit from the website. It was a hobby for her, and although it did earn a little bit of money, her main income was from her job.

Website buyers should be suspicious of situations like this one where the seller claims that they haven't attempted to monetize their website. The suspicion is justified because the majority of sellers who say that are lying. They have actually tried and failed. Buyers are worried that they will fail, too, so they limit the amount they are willing to bid.

However, the more I researched the site, using the methods I outline in this book, the more I liked the website. From everything I could see, she really hadn't attempted to milk earnings out of the site. I grew to believe that there was untapped revenue potential. The seller answered my scores of questions patiently and thoroughly. She gave me access to login and view the site's Google Analytics statistics. She shared tons of advice about what to do and what not to do to make the website grow and protect it from future threats. As the auction progressed, we developed a good working relationship, and both of us were happy when I had the winning bid.

One of my good friends had been itching to get in on the website investing game. He had been listening to my stories about website buys for months. When this one came along, I asked if he wanted in, and he was on board immediately.

How has this buy stacked up against my perfect-website-purchase wish list?

Goal: Low effort or no effort	Result: Low effort
Mandatory, ongoing maintenance is next to nothing, giving this purchase an excellent rating. There have been a few problems and improvement projects that generated work. Website outages prompted us to move the site to a different server. We worked to clean up a lot of "not found" links that pointed to non-existent pages. We changed the theme of the website to look better on mobile devices. We experimented with different ad placements and types. We have added a bit of new content.	

Goal: Low risk	Result: Some risk
There was a risk to the Adsense account when Google said they didn't like their ads placed on pages they considered "mature." These were pages like the one titled "Sex After Back Surgery." We removed all of them as soon as we were warned. Despite having high quality standards for SEO, we still lost some traffic in a Google algorithm change. There is an ongoing risk from new competition from other health sites.	

Goal: Long life	Result: Going strong
The website has maintained a healthy level of traffic. It has not lost value as an asset, meaning it could be sold for at least what we paid for it.	
Goal: Google resistant	Result: Sensitive to Google
It has not proven to be completely immune to Google changes. It continues to receive a majority of its traffic from Google, and the traffic levels change when Google changes its algorithms.	
Goal: Short payback period	Result: Acceptable
The payback period worked out to be fifteen months. Although this was higher than my target of ten months, the website is still earning a generous 6.5% monthly ROI, calculated as monthly net profit / website purchase rice. Because the website looks like it will have a long life and delivers consistent monthly cash flow, I am happy with the financial performance.	
Goal: High-quality service	Result: Excellent
Based on their comments, readers find the articles very helpful.	

2. Where Do You Find Websites for Sale?

A nswer: through online website brokers and online website marketplaces or by buying directly from the owner.

Website Brokers

Like all business brokers, website brokers represent the sellers of website businesses. Brokers prefer to specialize in the sale of high-priced websites. Some go for as low as $10,000, but most have minimums of $25,000, $50,000, or even $100,000.

This is by no means a comprehensive list of website brokers, but some of the popular ones include:

- AcquisitionsDirect.com
- DaltonsBusiness.com

- DigitalExits.com
- EmpireFlippers.com
- FEInternational.com
- FlipFilter.com
- Flippa.com (Deal Flow)
- Latonas.com
- QuietLightBrokerage.com
- TheWebsiteBrokers.com
- W3BusinessAdvisors.com
- WebsiteProperties.com
- WeSellYourSite.com

Unlike traditional brick and mortar business brokers, website brokers sell Internet properties whose assets are primarily digital. They understand the importance of certain metrics that are specific to websites, like traffic statistics, conversion rates, email open rates, and earnings per page view. They also understand revenue models that are frequently used by websites (such as pay per action, pay per click, subscriptions, etc.) and typical expenses and operational concerns.

"No great man ever complains of want of opportunity."

–Ralph Waldo Emerson

Dealing with a broker can sometimes be easier than communicating directly with a seller because brokers fundamentally understand what information is important to the buyer of a website. They can also assist you in the sales contract, escrow, and the transition process after there is agreement on price. However, brokers who interfere with direct communication between buyers and sellers or sellers who resist any direct communication are a problem.

It is very important to have direct conversations with a seller to get a sense for his or her integrity and willingness to provide support after a transaction is completed. Avoid brokers who don't facilitate a direct contact.

Asking prices for websites are almost always higher at website brokerages than at website marketplaces. This is primarily because high-value sites are older, have more stability, and enjoy less risk in their business models.

Does buying through a broker reduce the risk of ending up with a failing website? Yes. It's not that brokers frequently turn down opportunities to sell low-quality websites. It is more the case that brokers use a standardized process to collect and present a complete picture of website performance. Risks and opportunities are more clearly highlighted for potential buyers.

Marketplaces

Here are a few of the well-known marketplaces for buying and selling websites:

- BizBuySell.com
- BizSale.co.uk (UK focused)
- Businessesforsale.com
- eBay.com
- FlipFilter.com (aggregates auctions)
- Flippa.com
- Forums.Digitalpoint.com
- iMergeAdvisors.com
- Webmaster-talk.com
- WebsiteAcquire.com
- WebsiteBroker.com

Visit **HeckYeah.org** to get help finding buying opportunities.

Flippa

Flippa is by far the current leading marketplace. At the writing of this chapter in mid-2014, Flippa claims 2,275 open listings and $428,000 in sales over the past seven days. Although there may be a higher total sales volume at other brokerage houses because of the sale of high-priced businesses, Flippa is the undisputed leader in terms of raw numbers of sites sold. Many startups have tried to challenge Flippa's dominance in the website buy and sell market and have thus far failed to unseat the giant.

The Flippa website boasts an excellent user interface and the management team continues to revise and improve it every year. The company has focused specifically on adding features to protect buyers and sellers. These include some basic due diligence tools, like links to Alexa, SEMRush, Copyscape, and others. It also has a deal with Escrow.com, provides sample sales contracts, sample non-disclosure agreements, sophisticated search tools, good customer service, new user accounts verification, user profile integration with feedback mechanisms to establish buyer and seller reputations, and feedback on post-sale website performance. Flippa also offers tools that certify Google Analytics data and Google Adsense revenue streams, which are very commonly used by sellers as proof of traffic and revenue.

This is not intended to be a sales pitch specifically for Flippa.com. However, it is obligatory to recognize Flippa's position as the dominant marketplace in the space, especially for properties priced less than $50,000. I have personally done $170,000 in transactions with Flippa at the time of this writing. My fourteen-year-old son even browses Flippa, looking for gaming websites to buy.

Within the website investment community, Flippa has many critics and naysayers. Their principle objection is that many websites sold on Flippa are junk. This criticism spawns from the fact that Flippa sells thousands of low-end websites. Many of these websites are templates, copied and pasted content created for the sole purpose of being sold. Personally, I applaud entrepreneurs who have found a product that they can create repeatedly and sell consistently to a steady stream of buyers. However, those who increase sales by making false claims are another matter, and unfortunately, there are a fair number of those tricksters on Flippa as well.

A second criticism is that many sellers on Flippa are scammers. Although Flippa does its best to discourage illegitimate sellers, there are still sites for sale that do not actually receive the claimed level of revenue, profits, or traffic. Sellers may omit pertinent details or may, in fact, manufacture false documentation supporting sales expenses and traffic.

"Nowadays people talk about PayPal's founders as prescient geniuses who would inevitably change the world. It was, however, not so obvious that PayPal would taste its first major success by helping people sell Beanie Babies on eBay. But they had a vision, a hope, and the perseverance to try multiple iterations until they got it right."

–Eric Ries

Clearly this problem is not unique to Flippa, but because it has a large number of open listings and does not perform a manual review of each and every website, its listings are subject to the risk of being fraudulent. Of course, as an investor in websites or in any other investment opportunity, the burden is always on the buyer to fully investigate before a deal is reached.

Private Deals
In the past, it was often possible to find websites online and approach the owner by sending an email or filling out his online contact form

with an offer to buy. The owner of the website might not have given any thought to making a sale previously. Nevertheless, many sites were sold because a buyer reached out directly to the owner.

Website owners today are often inundated with unsolicited email. As a result, very few unexpected emails are opened, read, or given the slightest consideration. However, some people continue to use this technique, focusing particularly on sites that seem to have potential because they are under-monetized. If you want to try it, make sure that your initial letter explains who you are (anonymity won't help your case) and why you are interested. Ask questions gently and respectfully to assess the owner's potential interest in selling.

I do send email inquiries expressing interest in buying websites, but I rarely receive any responses from the owners.

One tactic to find websites for sale is to simply enter a Google search for phrases such as "this website is for sale" or "website for sale." If you take this approach, be prepared to sift through many sites that are not remotely interesting. But you never know when you might stumble upon a gem at a good price by going direct and avoiding competition.

Networking

Once you let it be known that you buy websites, word starts to get out. Attending conferences and building relationships with buyers of your sites and those you've bought sites from generates more opportunities to find sites for sale.

Deals spawned from relationships are often the most valuable. There is less competition and potentially more authenticity. There is less time pressure and may be more trust.

Of course, these deals happen by chance, so they are fewer and farther between. But the serious investor will advertise his interest in buying websites wherever he goes, and deals will eventually materialize.

Website Buying Groups

Much like stock investment clubs, groups of investors have begun to ban together to buy websites.

Below are a few of the advantages of buying websites as a group of investors:

1. Diversification: a group can own afford to own more properties.
2. Education: investors in a group can share experience and knowledge.
3. Buying power: high-priced websites are often unavailable to the new investor who can't afford them. Pooling resources allows investors to buy high-performing, less-risky website businesses.

How do you find a group to join? Network at Internet marketing conferences, or start your own group.

Case Study: Abracadabra

I've always loved magic. Even though I had never seriously considered being in the magic business, getting in on the act would be, for me, like finding a job as an ice cream taster. So when I found a magic website for sale that was actually making money, I was instantly interested in finding out all about it.

The website was the personal brainchild of a prolific magician who had performed more than four thousand shows before the age of twenty-nine. He was worn out and looking to get into a business that didn't require him to travel thirty days per month.

Visitors to the website were looking for a magician to perform at birthday parties for children, family gatherings, or corporate events. The site described the magician himself and the content of his shows; it also had some sample videos of his act. Visitors could fill out a form or call an 800 number to request a performance.

The magician had created the site to market himself and create bookings for his shows. As the site grew in search engine rankings, traffic picked up, and soon he was getting a lot more requests for shows than he could handle by himself. He began to send the extra leads to some of his magician buddies, who were grateful for them. They would pay him a cut after they did a show and received payment. They *usually* paid him, that is. It became a hassle for him to follow up with them, and he also started getting requests to do shows in faraway cities where he had no magician friends to whom he could give the leads.

Soon the magician decided to find another way to profit from the leads he was generating. He approached an entertainment broker who had given him leads in the past, and the broker was more than happy to buy the leads. The broker began paying him $4 per lead. Whether the visitor filled out the form on the website, sent an email, or called the 800 number, the magician received $4. In his peak month, he sold one thousand leads and made $4,000. His monthly costs for the website were less than $100.

This website met almost all of my criteria, so I dug in, looking for a catch but hoping that I wouldn't find one. The first obstacle was that he wasn't going to let it go for as little as I would have liked. (Keep in mind that I am on the cheap end of cheap.) But the package was so compelling I wasn't ready to let a little thing like price derail my plans to be in show business.

I kept thinking, "If that broker is so willing to pay $4 per lead, he is probably making a great deal more than that." The magician had provided a letter from the broker stating he would continue buy leads from the new website owner. Plans started developing in mind to keep more of the profits by managing my own network of magicians and eventually cutting the broker out. Shoot, I might even learn a few tricks myself.

The seller provided access to all kinds of information. He showed me phone logs, invoices, and emails. He gave me access to traffic statistics and showed me his PayPal account over a Skype screen-sharing session. I spent about three hours on the phone with him over the course of the auction. I was becoming very confident that this was going to be a winner.

Then came the red flag. While the magician was sharing his screen, we were looking at his Google Webmaster Tools account. The bad news came in the form of a message from Google that said they had levied a manual action against the entire website due to "unnatural links." The message was recent, and it meant that the website would get far, far less traffic from Google until the manual action from Google could be cleared.

After further research, it was apparent that traffic had begun to slow dramatically. Because it was a low season for magic shows, the impact on revenue had not yet become apparent. Although some of the website's traffic came directly from other websites, the impact of not having traffic from Google was severe enough to cause me to stop pursuing the opportunity.

3. Narrowing Down the Search

My students and consulting clients are initially overwhelmed by the sheer volume of buying opportunities. They simply don't know where to begin.

Some are better than others, but most brokerages and marketplaces offer the ability to search listings with specific criteria. In this chapter, we will discuss ways for you to narrow down the search for your next website.

Niches

In most sites, you can search by niche or by keyword. The niche search is often accurate because the seller has identified the website as belonging to a particular niche, like automotive, education, entertainment, etc. Keyword searches may yield unexpected results, highlighting some interesting websites that may have been categorized in a different niche than the one you were searching in.

If you have knowledge in a particular subject area, you may well want to evaluate websites that fit your knowledge base. I have a great deal of experience with Google News sites, so I have specific searches set up that alert me anytime another news site is put up for sale.

You can also search by characteristics such as private versus public auctions, site age, revenue, net profit, revenue sources, and traffic. I have generic searches established that notify me anytime a site is put up for sale that is at least twelve months old, earns $1,000 to $10,000 a month in profit, and has more than 20,000 unique visitors per month. This search consistently yields some interesting opportunities for me, but you will want to experiment to make sure your search is not giving you more or less options than what you need. For example, the search above may exclude a very profitable website that has low levels of traffic. It might also exclude websites that have a great deal of traffic but have not generated good revenue from the traffic.

Tip: Search for sites that have high traffic and low revenue. This can be an indicator of extra revenue potential. The site owner may have been successful at attracting high numbers of visitors, but deficient in making sales to those visitors.

Tip: Search for sites that have high revenue and low traffic. Sites in this category usually sell high-priced goods or services. They are often very good at converting a small number of visitors into sales. If you can increase traffic to these sites, there is potential for much greater levels of revenue.

Purpose

Your search criteria will be driven by your purpose for buying a website. At different times, in different situations, I have had a variety of reasons to buy, including the following:

- To earn income
- To increase my portfolio of websites in a particular niche
- To learn a new business model
- To capitalize on an undervalued web site
- To flip a website for profit
- To diversify my portfolio because I had too many sites dependent on traffic from Google
- To pick up a site in a subject area of interest

I set up search criteria for each different buying purpose. If you are working directly with a broker, he will most certainly want to understand your goals and your budget. Brokers can be very motivated to locate opportunities for you that meet your goals. However, brokers are salesmen. They have the dual goals of making their customers happy *and* making a sale. So don't be too surprised if brokers present opportunities that are not completely in line with your goals.

In the next chapter, we will talk extensively about the different kinds of business models websites use to make money. Knowing which business models are attractive to you will provide additional criteria you can use to narrow your search for the perfect website.

Let the Opportunities Come to You

Every brokerage, and most marketplaces like Flippa, send new "for sale" listings out by email. **Flipfilter.com** has the best advanced-search page available anywhere. This saves you the trouble of logging on to look for the new opportunities.

That's why I tell my students that the very first thing they should do is set up accounts with marketplaces and brokerages to start receiving short summaries. In fact, whether or not you've decided to buy your first website, I encourage you to visit the marketplaces listed in the chapter titled "Where Do You Find Websites to Buy?" and begin setting up some accounts now.

Seeing current website "for sale" listings come into your inbox is the best way to learn the kinds of websites available, the revenue models they use, and how much sellers are asking.

Flippa's Saved Search

Because Flippa has the largest volume, and therefore, the widest variety of sites for sale, make sure you create a Flippa account.

Earlier in this chapter, I described how you should define your search criteria. This is how you can set up the advanced search to email new listings to you:

Step 1
- At the Flippa.com website, click on <u>Sign Up</u>. Enter a username, email address, and password.
- After you have completed the account setup and verification steps, you can move on to Step 2.

Step 2
- Log in to your newly created account and click on <u>Advanced Search</u>.

Step 3
- Edit the search criteria and click <u>Search Listings.</u>

Step 4
- The search results page will appear. Click the blue button at the top of the page that says <u>Save This Search</u>.
- That's it. Flippa will now start sending you new listings that meet your search criteria.

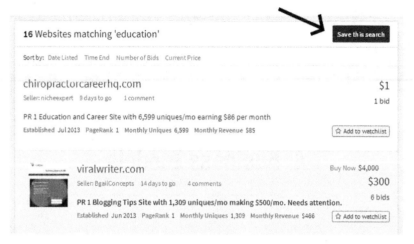

Flippa Search Results

4. Business Models

T his chapter explains in detail how websites make money. Read it top to bottom for a broad foundation, or skim to find the models that are of interest to you.

Advertising

In raw numbers, there are far more content websites than any other kind on the Internet. Content sites are those that attract visitors with their text and media content. These include blogs, news sites, video sites, forums, reference and resource sites, and many other categories. While any website can monetize itself in multiple ways, the majority of content sites make their money by some form of advertising. Advertising can be directly negotiated between a company and a publishing website, or it can be brokered through an advertising network or advertising agency.

Ad networks like Google Adwords have created powerful technology that manages hundreds of thousands of ad campaigns in real time. An advertiser creates an ad and specifies the keywords they will bid for. The ad will be displayed in search results or on content websites alongside content that is a fit for its keywords. Google's software analyzes the content of each web page and extracts keywords that are a match for companies whose campaigns are interested in those words.

Google then manages a real-time auction in which the company who has placed the highest bid for a particular keyword for a particular ad size will get first dibs on a particular website ad position. Google then automatically displays the ad on the publisher's website on behalf of the advertiser. That may sound complicated, but it is actually much more complicated than it sounds.

The net result of this evolving "contextual" ad technology is that websites can sign up for an Adsense account, and Google will maximize their ad revenue potential by placing the ads for them. Websites are paid on a per-click basis (CPC) or a per-impression basis (CPM). In the per-click model, a manufacturer, for example, might pay $1.50 for each click on one of its ads. Google might keep $0.50 and pass along $1 to the website owner. In the per-impression model, a company might pay $10 for every thousand times its ad is displayed on a website. Google might keep $4 of that and pass $6 along to the website owner.

In effect, Google and other sophisticated ad networks have made it extremely easy for website owners to earn money from their content websites.

Content websites produce very passive income streams, provided there is a steady stream of traffic. I own content websites that get a steady stream of visitors from articles I published long ago on sites that I have not updated in years. However, traffic is a fickle beast, and as many stories as there are about steady, long-term traffic, there are just as many about traffic that was there one day and dried up the next. More about traffic later, but for the purposes of our advertising discussion, be aware that if you are buying a website that earns its money from advertising, consistent traffic will either make or break your profitability.

"Financial peace isn't the acquisition of stuff. It's learning to live on less than you make, so you can give money back and have money to invest. You can't win until you do this."

—Dave Ramsey

Leading ad networks include Adwords, AdBrite, Adblade, 24/7 Open, AdStream, AdCenter, Ad Magnet, BuySellAds.com, Chitika, Clickbooth, DoubleClick, ExoClick, Infolinks, Yahoo! Publisher Network (and Bing), and Zedo. There are many private ad agencies and smaller ad networks as well. Websites might do much better using a particular ad agency in their niche and market than using a generic network. Some ad networks, like Tribal Fusion, require a minimum of five-hundred-thousand page views per month.

While there are always exceptional situations, Adsense tends to outperform other ad networks, hands down. In fact, whenever I look at sites using other networks exclusively, it raises a red flag for me; I question why Adsense is not being used. Many times the reason is because Adsense has decided the site content does not meet its standards, or the Adsense account holder has done something to violate its terms and conditions. If the site owner has simply never tried it, replacing other ads with Adsense might represent a good opportunity to increase ad revenue.

Targeted Content for Advertising Monetization

Because contextual ad networks read and understand the topic and keywords of each individual web page, smart content website owners intentionally create content that will attract ads with the biggest payouts. Do keep in mind that actual per-click earnings vary widely. Here are some broad categories of content and how ads typically perform on those webpages:

Legal Medical Procedures Business to Business Banking and Finance	$20 to $50 per 1,000 page views
Mobile Devices Other Technology Network and Computing Jobs Education Automobiles	$10 to $35 per 1,000 page views
Drugs and Medicine Science Web hosting Fitness Home and Garden Travel Dating	$5 to $25 per 1,000 page views
General News Sports Music Gaming Fashion and Clothing	$1 to $15 per 1,000 page views

The numbers in the table above are wide ranges of what can be expected. There are niches within these broad categories that can generate far higher returns—even at the lower levels of the chart. It is important to note that advertising spend is very dynamic and seasonal. Over 60% of ad dollars are spent during the holiday season in the last few months of the year. Products regularly come in and out of fashion, and the ad dollars associated with those products vary accordingly.

Tip: Content writers should consider their articles and media from a manufacturer's point of view. If I were a manufacturer or retailer, would I be happy if the ad for my product appeared on this web page? What products would this web page reader be interested in buying? What keywords would he be searching for that a manufacturer might also place an ad bid on?

The best content website creators start by understanding the products and advertising numbers associated with potential content and then create articles to attract the highest number of visitors and the highest revenue per click. Often articles on a topic with high paying ads like "personal injury attorneys" might not attract a great deal of search traffic, but the visitors who find the articles are more likely to click on an ad, and the ads they click on will have high per-click revenue. I have witnessed single clicks that paid as much as $40.

So what products tend to be the ones with both high traffic and high per-click revenue? That is the elusive and golden question. But consider Apple iPhones. The combination of the handset cost and a two-year contract with a telecommunication company often results in a total price of as much as $5,000 over that two years. Mobile providers are willing to pay several dollars per click for a potential sale of that size. So the per-click revenue meets the criteria, but what about traffic? Because Apple commands a 40%+ portion of market share in its space, search traffic is also excellent. Popularity + high price is the nirvana for content pages. Unfortunately, that is not a big secret, so there is extensive competition for those keywords. Many website owners experiment with pages about lesser known, but high-priced, products to write about. They test a variety of items until they locate niches that are under-exploited. We will discuss this more when we cover "low-hanging fruit" opportunities.

Direct Advertising

For websites that are very focused on a specific niche and want to monetize with advertising, approaching specific companies or specific ad agencies to negotiate paid ad space arrangements may be advantageous (compared to using the ad networks discussed above). Working directly with a distributor or manufacturer cuts out the middleman and leaves more profits for all. Manufacturers will typically pay per one-thousand impressions. So if the agreed rate is $10 per one-thousand impressions, that means the webpage with their creative (ad) would need to be shown to visitors one-thousand times in order for you to earn $10. That doesn't necessarily mean one-thousand unique visitors, since a visitor may view more than one page in a single visit to the website. There are a wide variety of tools available for tracking visits and page views, and many of them are free.

Affiliate Marketing

The work-at-home crowd is very familiar with the popular business model of affiliate marketing. Product creators create a product like a video course, ebook, training website, or coaching program, and then they recruit affiliates to sell the product in exchange for a commission on every sale. It is typically very easy to sign up to be an affiliate for almost anything, although some affiliate programs have requirements related to how many sales you have made in the past and the methods you will use to market the product.

Once you are approved as an affiliate, you are free to advertise the affiliate product and attract customers to buy the product via your referral link. When a visitor clicks your link and purchases a product, you receive commissions for the sale.

Hundreds of thousands of websites and millions of web pages have been created exclusively for the purpose of selling affiliate products. Not surprisingly, literally hundreds of books have been written about how to do affiliate marketing. This is appealing to many people who want to start an Internet business quickly because it does not require the creation of a unique product to sell.

The savvy website buyer can sometimes find affiliate websites that already have a consistent traffic base and an affiliate product that converts well. This allows him to bypass the work of researching affiliate products, creating a website, and attracting traffic that is likely to buy the product.

Affiliate websites typically consist of landing pages that are pre-sales pages. They contain persuasive content or reviews about a particular product that warm up customers to the idea of buying. Then if the customer clicks on the "call-to-action" button, they are directed to the sales page created by the product creator, who hopes to close the sale. Affiliate programs promise to track the customers with reliability and integrity so that the affiliate is confident he will get paid for any visitor he sends to the sales page.

"One secret of success in life is for a man to be ready for his opportunity when it comes."

—Benjamin Disraeli

The two primary goals of the affiliate marketer are to attract as many visitors to his pages as possible and to influence as many of those visitors as he can to click through to the final sales page. The first goal is about traffic creation, and we will discuss that in a later chapter, but broadly speaking, there are two categories of traffic: paid and organic. Paid traffic is visitors received from advertising sources that have been paid for. Organic traffic is free visitors that have come from search engines, social networks, and emails. It also includes direct visitors who are aware of the website and type in the URL or have it bookmarked in their browsers.

The second goal of influencing visitors to click through to the final sales page is all about salesmanship and copywriting. The affiliate marketer usually takes the tactic of informing, not selling. He presents reviews, facts, and sometimes testimonials about a product with the intent of creating a positive curiosity that leads the customer to take the next step. The hard selling, where sales copy plays on the intellect and emotions of the buyers in a more overt way, is left to the final sales page. The final sales page is on the product creator's website. This is where prices and guarantees are revealed.

The entire sales process—or sales funnel, as it is commonly called—may include the following:

1. An ad where the Internet user is first presented with a product or topic
2. A landing page where the user is informed about the topic and encouraged to proceed further
3. A sales page offering more information where the user is "sold" on the product
4. A download page granting access to the purchased product and additional, complimentary products called "upsells"
5. A downsell page where customers who have chosen not to purchase are given another offer, most often lower in price with fewer features
6. A squeeze page where customers are offered something free in exchange for providing their email addresses

There are thousands of variations on sales funnel structures. There may be multiple levels of upsells and downsells or none at all. Visitors and buyers will almost always be encouraged to provide an email address or contact information so that they can be placed on a "leads" email list or a "buyers" email list. Once they are on a list, they will receive frequent emails that attempt to sell additional products.

Services

A large number of websites exist by selling services. As the word *service* implies, the owner of these websites must welcome ongoing effort and interaction with customers.

"High-touch" websites include such services as design, programming, writing, advertising, SEO, research, translation, and thousands more. High-touch services are most often sold by the project or by the hour.

"The older I get, the more I see a straight path where I want to go. If you're going to hunt elephants, don't get off the trail for a rabbit."

—T. Boone Pickens

"Low-touch" websites offer partially automated services, like background checks, link building, business listings, and anything where programs and tools have been developed to do most, but not all, of the work involved in delivering the service. These services are often sold per transaction.

There are also many service businesses that are almost fully automated. I recently reviewed a website that was an online tool for the creation of business plans. The website led the user through a series of questions and provided guidance and resources along the way. The end result was a professional-looking, but completely self-service, business plan.

There are also websites that do well by providing multiple levels of service. The lower levels are automated and have lower price points, and the higher levels receive more human interaction and have higher prices. For many years, I have co-owned a health site that presents a client with an exhaustive survey of over nine-hundred questions about diet, lifestyle, and health concerns. The lowest cost output of the website is a seventy- to one-hundred-page health report that is completely computer generated. It is ingenious in its ability to identify hard-to-diagnose health conditions. For those who want a doctor's input, a higher priced report is available, which includes a doctor's review of the questionnaire results and customized notes from the doctor.

Incidentally, this health website is also a content website. It has hundreds of pages of information about treatments and conditions and attracts traffic from Google and Bing. Visitors to the website generate both ad revenue and services revenue if they choose to sign up for a health report.

A Quick Word on Outsourcing

Those looking for passive revenue should not necessarily ignore service-based websites because there are many situations where the work can easily be outsourced. Consider a logo design website. The owner of the website receives an order for a new logo. He then sends the requirements to a low-cost designer who creates the logo and sends it back to the owner. In this scenario, the owner's only action is the handoff between the customer and the outsourced labor. Even this interaction can be minimized or eliminated with the right automated systems.

eCommerce—Selling Physical Products

Who sells $47,000 per minute online at this writing? Amazon.com, that's who.

More money changes hands on the Internet from eCommerce websites than any other category. All eCommerce websites are concerned with selling physical (or digital) products, and money is received when a sale is processed or when the goods are shipped (or downloaded). eCommerce sites are successful under these conditions:

1. They attract visitors to their website.
2. They convince visitors to buy.
3. They provide a satisfactory product.
4. They provide satisfactory service pre- and post-sale.

Shipping

Either the website packages and ships products themselves, or the manufacturer or distributor drop ships the product to the customer on behalf of the website. Self-shipping of products may potentially increase profitability because the seller may get a better price for inventory from the wholesaler. However, self-shipping means that the website owner must do the following:

1. Buy inventory
2. Stock and measure inventory levels
3. Package product for shipment
4. Ship product
5. Manage returns

These responsibilities require effort and good systems. The fewer product types being sold, the easier it is to manage.

Drop Shipping

As eCommerce has exploded and continues to grow at double-digit rates every year, manufacturers of small items, like medicine and jewelry, and big items, like furniture and automobiles, offer drop-shipping services. For the website owner, drop shipping saves many headaches. The website becomes a pure middleman; its main function is to attract customers, take and track orders, and place those orders with the manufacturer. That doesn't mean drop-ship eCommerce sites are necessarily easy to operate, but it does mean they can be operated without ever touching the product.

Amazon

Working with Amazon—instead of competing with Amazon—is a strategy many thousands of people have adopted over the past ten years. However you choose to engage with Amazon, they hold almost all the cards. They own and keep the customers (they don't give you customer contact information, for example); they own customer service and make product return decisions on your behalf; they choose what to sell and what not to sell; and they influence pricing. Amazon lets you in on their game, but it is no secret that the giant is in the driver's seat. The reason they can do this—and the reason you may still want to work with them—is that the site has a massive customer base. Working with Amazon gives you access to far greater numbers of customers than you could ever hope to attract on your own.

One way to work with Amazon is simply to buy ads. If you are selling a particular shoe, Amazon might show your ad to buyers who have opened a product page for that shoe or other items connected to what you are selling.

"My experience indicates that most people who've accumulated a great deal of wealth haven't had that as their goal at all. Wealth is only a by-product, not the original motivation."

–Michael Milken

Another way to work with Amazon is to sell on Amazon. That means you offer products that Amazon is either already selling or not selling. If they already sell the product, there is an existing sales page with images and sales copy about the product. If that doesn't exist, you create your own product page. When a customer buys your product, Amazon informs you, and you ship the product to the customer. Amazon takes a percentage of the sale price of each item sold.

To further simplify the process, you may mail your product inventory to an Amazon distribution center. Under Amazon's Fulfillment By Amazon (FBA) program, they will ship products to customers on your behalf. Amazon charges you for this service—in addition to the fees for selling your product on its website.

eBay

eBay is, of course, the other monster in the eCommerce space, and it is responsible for making the auction format for buying goods pervasive. eBay store websites do not pop up for sale very often, but it certainly does happen.

Leads

Selling leads can be golden. I have encountered some fascinating examples of websites that collect information and then sell that information as leads to interested parties.

One website I evaluated for purchase provided information to readers about a rare medical condition. The website had about fifteen pages of content and attracted about fifteen-hundred visitors per month. On each page of the website, there was an invitation for the reader to enter his or her name and mailing address to be sent a free information packet with more extensive information about the medical condition. The website owner sent out approximately thirty of those information packets per month. He sold those thirty leads to a medical malpractice attorney for $125 each. The attorney was happy to buy 360 leads a year for a few potential cases that could yield millions of dollars in legal fees.

Recapping from an earlier story, a magician was selling his website that showcased his talents and invited visitors to schedule him for magic shows at birthday parties and corporate events. He began to receive many more leads for shows than he could possibly perform himself. He began to sell each of those leads to an entertainment broker who paid $4 for each lead. The leads came in the form of phone calls, contact forms, and emails. He received $4—regardless of the format of the lead. The broker was happy to pay the $4 because he knew that a high percentage of those leads could result in magic show bookings of $300 to $800 each.

Subscriptions

Subscriptions or membership websites are akin to content websites in that they sell information. However, subscription websites require membership enrollment, and the content is only available to paid members. My coaching program at HeckYeah.org is an example of a subscription-based service.

> Subscription websites are attractive because the income stream from a customer continues each month.

Online newspapers now sell subscriptions, just as their physical counterparts have done for years. Training websites are often subscription based. Members have access to courses, papers, videos, programs, tools, forums, and private marketplaces. Subscription websites are attractive because the income stream from a customer continues each month. Each new customer has much more potential value than if you were selling a product with a one-time fee.

Email Marketing

Email is widely used as a method to drive customers to websites where they are encouraged to buy a product or service. Websites using email as a primary traffic source may be more stable than those dependent on search-engine traffic.

Email addresses are collected by displaying a "squeeze page." Squeeze pages are full website pages or sections of pages that offer something for free in exchange for a name and email address. Free giveaways include things like newsletters, ebooks, white papers, or videos. They are almost always digital, so there is no cost to the owner to capture the email address.

Vendors like Aweber, MailChimp, and GetResponse manage email databases and email delivery so that website owners can focus on the email message content and not the mechanics. To see the tools I use, visit **HeckYeah.org/resources**.

Some websites build email lists to have an incremental sales channel. Their primary product may be sold on a website, while accessories are marketed to the list. Other websites build lists and use them to remind customers of its brand. These sites consistently provide useful, free content to the list and regularly entice customers to click on links back to the main website where new products are offered for sale.

Comparison of Revenue Sources

The website investor doesn't consider any particular business model better than another but recognizes unique advantages and risks inherent in each model. Determining which business models are more appealing in view of your skills and preferences and which are in better alignment with your goals can be a big help in narrowing the search for your next website purchase. The chart below compares characteristics of revenue sources, but it is only a general guide since every website is unique:

Revenue Source	Work Requirement per Transaction	Systems Requirement	Knowledge Requirement
Advertising – Contextual	Low	Low	Low
Advertising – Direct	Low to Medium	Low	Low
Affiliate	Medium	Low	Medium
Services – High Touch	High	Low	High
Services – Low Touch	Medium	Medium	Medium
Services – No Touch	Low	High	Medium
eCommerce – Self Shipping	Medium	High	Medium
eCommerce – Drop Shipping	Low	Medium	Low
eCommerce – Partner with Amazon or eBay	Low to High	Low to Medium	Medium
Leads	Low	Medium	Low
Subscriptions	Low	High	Medium

Case Study: Me, a Media Mogul

I sat fascinated, listening to a webinar hosted by successful Internet marketer, and now friend, Eric Holmlund. His guest was a guy who was extolling the virtues of Google News sites. Having your website recognized by Google News as an official news source gives your articles the opportunity to have first-page-search-engine rankings within five minutes after they are published, he said. He showed a live example on the webinar where he published an article with a valuable keyword phrase: "college scholarships." True to his word, it was picked up and available, high in the search results, about ten minutes later while we were still watching. He was selling a course for $500 that would reveal how to get into the news business and start raking in the dough.

Having cut my teeth in the corporate world, I am conditioned to ask the buy/build question in most project scenarios: Would it be better to buy the course, build my own website, request approval from Google, and if accepted, work to earn money from it? Or should I try to buy a site that is already approved by Google and making money?

If there had been nothing available to buy, I probably would have attempted to go it on my own. But I did find a site or two that had been newly accepted by Google News and had already started collecting traffic and revenue. So I bought in.

I paid $3,500 for the selected website, and the seller was a very savvy business guy who taught me everything he knew about running a Google News site. I began writing news articles myself and soon got into a rhythm that earned me $1,000 in the first full month. I got tired of writing articles, so I hired a freelancer to write for me. See how to outsource in the section "Getting Help" in the chapter titled "It's Mine; Now What?" I paid him $2.50 per 250 word article, and for that price, he would write the article, post it on the website, and find a picture to go with it. In that first year, I found a number of good writers—and a few not so good ones—willing to work within those terms.

I sent emails to the writers each evening, telling them what to write about and what keywords to emphasize in their titles and articles. I became skilled at figuring out which kinds of articles attracted the most traffic and which ones had the highest payouts per click on an ad. The website paid for itself in the first three months and grew to earn about $2,500 in net profit in its better months. There were other perks too. For example, the communications director of Tesla Motors offered to let me take the company's all-electric, $150,000 Tesla Roadster for a spin on the test track in California following articles we published about the new car.

Ten months after I purchased that first news site, Google decided that the articles we were publishing did not meet its editorial standards. They de-syndicated the website from Google News, and traffic immediately dropped by about 90%. Nevertheless, with no articles published in four years, money is still trickling in from that website every month. Google was justified in its decision, and I learned the balance between running after high-paying news content and maintaining journalistic standards.

The news story is still in progress. After the demise of the first news website, I bought others. I learned to build them from scratch and earn approval from Google. Some I sold, and others I continue to operate.

My wife homeschools our kids. As a school project, she decided to have them go through the course I created on how to get into Google News. I watched proudly as they created the website, outsourced the design, and recruited writers. Ultimately, the site was submitted to Google for syndication and accepted. It continues to contribute to the family's income to this day.

I now have excellent, experienced writers who pick their own topics and publish their own articles on my websites every day. This income is very passive, and the websites are solid performers in my portfolio.

5. Evaluating a Website

Buying a website is a lot like buying clothes, a car, or a house. You start by browsing, and then when a few things catch your eye, you dig deeper and start asking the seller and yourself a lot of tough questions. Questions that you ask yourself are as important as those you ask the seller. Here are some of the questions I regularly ask myself:

- Am I willing to do the work this website requires to maintain or grow its earnings?
- Am I interested in the subject area of this website?
- Do I have the right skills and desire to do the kind of work required? If it requires marketing, copywriting, programming, cold selling, administration, design, email writing, analysis, or research, can I do those things? Do I want to?

- Am I comfortable with the level of risk inherent in this website? Do I even know what the risks are?
- Is there anything objectionable about this website, its products, its customers, its suppliers, or the seller?
- Do I completely understand how this website gets its traffic and earns its revenue?

The possible questions are infinite, but if the website has a significant cost or work requirement, it's important to determine whether you are a good fit for the website.

Source Documents

Sellers need to produce proof to back up their claims of earnings, traffic, expenses, and everything else. They often provide screenshots as proof. Screenshots are images, and they can be faked easily. You can use screenshots to get an initial impression of the website, but if you are serious about buying it, you must eventually ask for more definitive proof.

Some sellers take a screen-capture movie that shows themselves logging into their Analytics, PayPalPayPal, Bank, or other accounts to prove the website statistics. These videos can also be faked, but it is much more difficult. A common technique is to ask the seller to share his screen with you over Skype or Teamviewer and show you exactly what you want to see, in real time, on the seller's PC.

"Sometimes your best investments are the ones you don't make."

—Donald Trump

Some kinds of accounts, like Google Analytics, will allow for the creation of a "read only" guest account. Most honest sellers are happy to add your gmail account to their Analytics accounts so that you can browse the historical and current statistics at your leisure. Another technique is to ask the seller to add your Amazon, Analytics, or Adsense code to his website for a period of time and then watch the actual sales and traffic metrics in your own account.

Ownership

How do you know if someone actually owns the site he is trying to sell? Marketplaces like Flippa verify ownership by having the seller upload a file to the website. The logic is that if the seller has enough access to put a file on the website, then he probably owns the website. That is a good sign, but it's useful to do more checking.

You can check http://who.is to find out the owner of the domain. If the domain is owned by a different name than the seller of the website, then that discrepancy needs to be clarified with the seller before you move forward. If who.is says that the domain has privacy protection, then the actual owner information will not be available publically. The seller should be able to show you information from his registrar account that demonstrates he is the rightful owner.

Tip: Avoid buying websites with another company's name or product name in the domain name. Using trademarked names, regardless of seller assurances that he's never had a problem, leaves you open to legal action.

Revenue

When someone says, "This is ten-million-dollar company," it is understood that they are talking about sales. The most important initial measure of a business is its revenue. We base our valuation of a site in large part on net income, not revenue. However, revenue numbers are critical because they reveal the size of the business, the appetite for the product or service, and the source of the customers.

You must know where every dollar of sales comes from. Is it from product sales or ads? Is it from services or leads? Is it paid via credit card? If so, is there a merchant account? And does that account come with the purchase of the site? Are payments made via PayPal or Moneybookers or 2Checkout or someone else? Do revenue accounts transfer over as part of the sale? If not, are there any restrictions or potential problems setting up your own accounts?

Are there any ongoing payments from existing customers? Are those payment streams part of the sale of the website? If so, how? Will the account be transferred, or is the seller expecting you to contact customers and ask them to renew under your PayPal account? For subscription customers, how long does the average customer stay subscribed? Is the duration two months, six months, or eight months?

What are the pricing tiers of products, and what is included for each tier? Is there a refund policy? How many refunds are there per month, and what percentage of customers ask for a refund?

The purpose for all these questions is to determine what the exact sales have been over time so you can accurately project what they will be in the future. From sales and expenses, you will be able to determine expected net profits. You must have an accurate forecast for net profits in order to know how much you are willing to bid on the website.

To help answer the questions above, the seller may provide any of the following as part of the listing:

- Account statements from revenue sources
- Bank account records
- Payment gateway statements (e.g. from PayPal or 2Checkout)
- Transaction logs
- Sales logs from eCommerce shopping carts

- Affiliate commission statements
- Profit and loss statements (P&L's); sometimes called income statements

One important technique for auditing revenue is to compare source documents to each other. Often the seller will provide a total revenue figure by month in the sales listing or prospectus. He may often also provide a profit and loss statement (P&L). Does the listing total match the P&L by month? If not, what is missing, or what is inflated? Do the detailed transactions in transaction logs, bank accounts, or PayPalPayPal registers add up to the totals in the listing and P&L? If a specific sale was $47.83 in one document, can you find that same sale for that exact same amount in other documents provided by the seller?

Studying these numbers doesn't take as much time as it sounds and can save a lot of heartache in the future. With this kind of analysis, you can accomplish the following:

- Uncover scams
- Uncover additional revenue sources the seller neglected to mention
- Uncover revenue risks, like declining subscriptions, high refund rates, or declining revenue per click
- Uncover the dependencies the website has on certain kinds of transactions or certain kinds of website traffic

Wouldn't it be good to know if 95% of the sales are from the German copy of the eBook and only 5% are from the English copy? Wouldn't it be a shock to find out too late that everyone was paying for live webinars, which require a time investment, instead of buying the pre-recorded video course?

For-sale listings in Flippa allow the seller to upload any documents he chooses. Flippa provides a tool for sellers to be able to certify earnings from Adsense ads. This is a very useful feature that immediately adds credibility to any listing that takes advantage of it. Unfortunately, it only exists for Adsense. One very useful validation technique is to request a screen-sharing session with the seller. Using a platform like Skype or Teamviewer, the seller can log into his financial accounts and go screen to screen showing you revenue records and transaction logs (as well as expense info and traffic analytics). Legitimate sellers should have no reason not to do this. If a seller refuses to do live, online screen sharing, it is an indication that maybe he or she has something to hide. Because this takes an investment in time and exposes the seller to some degree, I only make this request after I am serious about the possibility of purchasing the website.

If you are working through a brokerage, it is prudent to ask the broker what steps have been taken to insure that the revenue stated in the listing is accurate and complete. Answers may vary. It is also perfectly reasonable—and even expected—to request source documentation for all of the claimed revenue. It might seem like a scary prospect to do your own auditing of the website's financial information. But if it is too difficult for you to evaluate the financials before you buy the site, what's going to happen after you buy the site? For large website purchases, you should consider hiring a firm that specializes in due diligence. Centurica is one such company that focuses on the online business and tech startup space. I also help my clients evaluate websites at **HeckYeah.org**.

Evaluating the revenue for a website might take five minutes, five hours, or five days, depending on the size of the website, the complexity of the earnings sources, and how good the documentation from the seller is. This crucial first step will take you a long way toward deciding whether the website is what it claims to be and whether it is for you.

"I will tell you how to become rich. Close the doors. Be fearful when others are greedy. Be greedy when others are fearful."

—Warren Buffett

Sites with long, consistent revenue streams are more valuable than those with short sales histories. A longer track record probably indicates a loyal customer base or readership—or at least a proven process for consistently attracting customers. It indicates the website or website owner's ability to defend successfully against competition and succeed in the constantly changing technology and search-engine environment.

I worked for a furniture store in high school. The owner was constantly looking for new revenue streams to supplement furniture sales. As a result, we delivered furniture, installed air conditioners, set up waterbeds, rented out U-Haul trucks and trailers, and installed appliances.

Many website owners do the same thing. They start grasping at ideas to earn extra money from the website and soon end up with a laundry list of sources. You will find sites with affiliate sales, direct email marketing, Adsense, text link ads, eBook sales, paid guest posts, and any number of other things. I tend to shy away from sites that have too many revenue sources. Here are a few of my reasons:

- It may indicate that the seller has already squeezed every dime out of the site.
- Each revenue stream is an account or relationship that needs to be monitored and cared for.

- Visitors tend to get confused or repulsed by endless schemes to take their money.
- The seller may have focused on sales over customer experience, meaning he invested in content or product without making customer satisfaction a priority.

Expenses

Many website owners don't look at their websites as businesses. As a result, when the owner decides to sell a website, it becomes apparent that he doesn't know what it costs to operate the website or hasn't tracked the expenses. Like the revenue analysis, the goal of expense analysis is to know what all the expenses have been and what they are likely to be in the future. This will allow you to have as accurate a view of past and future net income as possible.

With expenses, you start with what the seller is claiming and test that against what you know about the business model of the website. Does the website ship product? If so, there should be packaging, postage, and perhaps storage costs. There should be the cost of purchasing the inventory. There should be the cost of processing returns. Think about each step needed to fulfill a sale on the website. What tools, services, and assets are needed to accomplish those tasks? If you don't find expenses recorded for each of those expected costs, the seller better have a good explanation. When you uncover a potential missing expense, the seller may very well have a legitimate reason for not including it in the P&L. Maybe the cost of packaging was already included in the cost of product purchases. Maybe the seller had a coupon for free Adwords advertising for the month.

"In investing, what is comfortable is rarely profitable."

–Robert Arnott

However, be wary of situations where the seller is getting something for free that you won't get for free. If the seller's nephew does SEO for him; or if he uses office supplies from his brick and mortar shop; or he makes one advertising payment for ads across three different websites; or he receives a free service that is no longer free for new accounts. . . or, or, or. You get the idea. You will need to estimate these expenses and factor them into your analysis.

Look for indicators of expenses on the website. Is there an 800 number listed on the website? It is unlikely that is free. Is there a chat system? Did you find banner ads for the website but no expense recorded for advertising? Does it look like multiple people are providing support or services for the website, but there is no labor expense listed?

Are product (cost of goods sold) costs and service costs actually what they are claimed to be? The seller should be able to produce invoices that show what he paid for services like programming, design, writing, and everything else. He should be able to produce a price schedule for products he is selling from the manufacturer that corresponds to the number of units he has purchased and the amount of expense he has recorded for cost of goods sold.

This is not meant to be a treatise on financial auditing techniques, because it is surely lacking if it were. The principle I emphasize is that you must think critically about the financial information claims of the website seller. It is really not important that the company books balance to the penny. It is important that the seller is not trying to mislead you and that you are not willing to mislead yourself about what the true expenses of the website will be.

Estimating the Cost of Your Time Invested

Depending on what kind of website you are evaluating, estimating the cost of time investment may be critical or may be unimportant. Website owners are notorious for underreporting the amount of time they invest in their websites. Take for example a website that earns $500 per month. The owner claims the only expenses are website hosting, which costs $12 per month. When you ask how much time he spends supporting the site, he responds four to six hours per week. That means there is a labor cost of between seventeen and twenty-six hours per month. If you have to pay someone $10 per hour to do what the owner currently does himself, the true net income of the website might not be $488/mth, but $228/mth instead. The value of the website might be less than half what it appears on paper.

"How many millionaires do you know who have become wealthy by investing in savings accounts? I rest my case."

—Robert G. Allen

Another concern is that website owners <u>don't really know</u> how much time they spend supporting their websites. How could they not know? A better question is how could they possibly know unless they tracked it in a systematic way? I have never met a website seller who could show me a detailed accounting of the time he or she spends supporting a website. He can show hours billed by paid contractors, but owners often neglect to log the personal time spent supporting the site.

It might very well be the case that you are willing to put in any amount of time necessary to run the business, in which case you might not be disturbed by an ill-defined time requirement. However, it is actually quite important that you are aware of the time requirement *and* the potential cost of labor when you make your buying decision.

I bought a site that sold software. I found that the majority of the work I could do myself. Although I didn't particularly enjoy doing the work, the earnings were worth the time investment. But there were a few times when a programmer was required to fix something. I found that the complexity and history of the software limited the choices I had for programmers. I also found that the best programmer for the job was also very expensive. Although this finding reduced my overall profits, I was fortunate not to require the programmer's services very often.

Financial Risk

It is impossible to catalogue an exhaustive list of financial risks an Internet business might encounter. Below is a list of events I have experienced with my own websites or that I have seen happen to other website investors:

- Price changes by competitors
- Products going out of style
- Unexpected taxes
- Changes in the cost of materials and services
- Unexpected legal fees
- Unexpected labor costs
- Costs of solving problems from pre-existing customers (those you inherited with the website)
- Inexperience in managing advertising campaigns
- Unexpected refund costs
- Changes in affiliate sales volume
- Suppliers deciding no longer to do business with you
- Cancelled accounts as a result of terms of service violations

There are, of course, many other kinds of operational risks, and we will touch on those in the following sections of this chapter.

Evaluating Customers

Websites are no less dependent on their customers than physical businesses. When I buy a website, I try to understand who the customers are that purchase the products and services of the business. It may be important to find out where they are, how old they are, how much they have to spend, how frequently they purchase, why they visit this website, why they purchase from this website, and what other things they might want to purchase.

Is the customer base stable? Do the same customers return and make repeat purchases? Is customer loyalty 100% or 0%?

Are customers connected to the website itself or to the persona of the current owner? Will the website lose customers when the ownership changes? Does the current owner use his own face or name on the website or in communications with customers? If so, is the owner willing for you to continue to use his name if you so choose?

We will talk about traffic in the next section, but we want to know which traffic source delivers the bulk of the paying customers. Then we want to know whether that traffic source is sustainable and whether we can grow it.

Evaluating customers isn't as high a priority as evaluating the financial aspects of the business, but for some websites, it is the key to understanding the growth potential for the website. Conversely, it may also highlight potential downside risk.

Traffic

Websites don't make money without traffic, just like businesses don't make money without customers. Second in importance to evaluating the financials of a website is understanding its traffic.

We want to know whether the existing traffic will remain stable, grow, or shrink. We want to know where traffic is coming from. Is it Google, Facebook, Pinterest, paid ads, other websites linking to this website, emails, bookmarks, or something else? We want to know if the traffic originates in Mongolia where the earnings per click are $0.03 or the UK where they are $0.30. We want to know how much traffic there is and how confident we can be that the traffic figures are accurate. We want to know what effort and money is required to keep the existing traffic coming and what the cost and effort will be to grow the traffic.

It is useful to compare traffic graphs to revenue graphs. Generally the two track together. If the traffic and revenue are going in different directions for certain periods of time or there is no clear correlation, it's something you need to investigate. Be particularly aware if the seller made changes described below:

- Changes that resulted in more targeted traffic: sales might be up when traffic is down.
- Changes to increase sales conversions: sales might be up without a change in traffic.
- Changes to pricing levels: sales might be up or down without a change in traffic.

Onsite Analytics Tools

Analytics tools are pieces of software that sit on the website and count visitors, page views, time spent on the site, and many other things. Google Analytics is the most commonly used tool because it is free and provides comprehensive statistics.

No tool provides perfectly accurate counts of visits and page views. Part of the dilemma is that many analytics tools make use of JavaScript, which may be disabled by some users or disrupted in certain circumstances. Another challenge is that there is a great deal of non-human traffic in the form of web bots, crawlers, and scrapers that might look like legitimate human visits from the perspective of certain tools. And, of course, the other problem is agreeing on the definitions of what constitutes a visitor, a unique visit, a page view, etc. and measuring those statistics in a consistent way. As you have probably guessed, no two measurement tools ever yield the same numbers. And to compound the problem, there is a wide variety of tools available and in common use.

Because Google is ubiquitous and because Google Analytics is completely free, a large percentage of websites use it. Some website owners don't use Analytics because they don't want to give Google access to any more information than it already has. Others believe there are superior tools out there and use those. Still others don't do any measuring at all, or they may choose to use whatever comes with their web-hosting plan, which is very often Awstat.

It is common for website sellers to operate a website for years without using any tracking tools and then find that they have made a big mistake when they put the website up for sale. Serious buyers won't bid without seeing accurate Analytics data.

Google Analytics is common enough that Flippa has built a system for verifying Google Analytics statistics. If a Google Analytics report is marked as certified in Flippa, it means that there is a reasonably strong probability that the report contains statistics that did indeed come from the website being sold. The obvious implication of that statement is that unverified Analytics are subject to being faked by unscrupulous website sellers. You also see that I did not completely vouch for Flippa's verification process because I have not studied the possibility of its system being duped, and I wouldn't dismiss that possibility. However, for my purposes, I have found it an adequate safeguard.

Offsite Traffic Tools

Other websites keep an eye on statistics as well. Because they do not actually have access to every website they watch, their data is an educated guess, extrapolated from the data they do have access to. I describe several of these tools below:

- **Alexa.com** ranks website traffic volume by country and also globally. It also reports on visitor demographics, keyword searches, and visitor engagement. Pro members have access to more statistics with greater accuracy.
- **SEMrush.com** reports competitors, ad statistics, keywords, and traffic. More data is available to pro subscribers.
- **Compete.com** reports traffic, visitor demographics, keywords, and traffic sources. Like the other sites, pro accounts provide more data.

It is definitely worth the time to pop in the URL you are evaluating and see what these tools have to say as part of your traffic research.

Source / Medium ?	Acquisition	
	Visits ? ↓	% New Visits ?
	1,235,766 % of Total: 100.00% (1,235,766)	**91.14%** Site Avg: 91.13% (0.02%)
1. google / organic	**598,725** (48.45%)	90.73%
2. (direct) / (none)	**258,509** (20.92%)	89.15%
3. news.google.com / referral	**141,966** (11.49%)	90.89%
4. bing / organic	**47,926** (3.88%)	92.41%
5. zergnet.com / referral	**33,615** (2.72%)	93.77%
6. facebook.com / referral	**21,297** (1.72%)	96.88%
7. m.facebook.com / referral	**19,808** (1.60%)	94.58%
8. google.com / referral	**10,255** (0.83%)	92.65%
9. blog.firmwareumbrella.com / referral	**9,695** (0.78%)	97.91%
10. google.de / referral	**8,766** (0.71%)	97.00%

Traffic Sources Shown in Google Analytics

Traffic Sources

Diagram 4 shows how Google Analytics identifies traffic sources.

- Google/Organic traffic is visits that came directly from the Google search results page.
- (Direct)/(None) includes visitors who typed in a URL directly in their browser, those who had bookmarked the page, and those where the original source of the traffic is unknown.
- News.Google.Com/Referral is traffic that comes from Google's news aggregation portal. You would only see this if the website is an official news source included in Google News.
- Bing/Organic is, of course, Microsoft's search engine.
- Other specific blogs, social networks, and search engines like Facebook, Reddit, Twitter, and all the rest are also tracked individually.

It is useful to look at the percentage of traffic from each source to understand the most important sources. Looking at each source over time gives you an idea as to which are growing or shrinking.

As we do with financial information, we also compare traffic source reports against each other when analyzing traffic. For example, I very often compare the page views reported on Google Adsense reports to those reported in Google Analytics reports. While they never match exactly, if they are within 10% of each other, I consider that good enough. If the seller also provides Clicky, Awstat, or a Wordpress plugin report, you can cross-reference those to see if any are in serious disagreement. If so, the first step is to question the seller about it and see if he responds with a reasonable explanation.

The more traffic history a seller can produce, the better. I am always suspicious of sites with only a month or two of traffic stats. The seller may have legitimate reasons for not being able to produce the data, but it gives you a lot less to go on. As a result, you should not place as high of a value on the website as you might have if it had a more lengthy sample of stats.

Get the website seller to give you view-only access to his Analytics accounts. Have him show you traffic statistics in a Skype or TeamViewer session. Sellers unwilling to do either of those things should be held in suspicion. If you are still keen on the website, at a bare minimum, demand to get copies of detailed reports from the analytics systems if the reports provided in the listing were insufficient.

Look for Strange Patterns

Traffic analysis is a bit dodgy. There are lots of things that can go wrong in the website world that affect traffic stats. Web-hosting servers go down. Websites go down. There are seasonal traffic patterns. There are weekly traffic patterns. There are traffic spikes caused by posts going viral on Facebook, by press releases, by breaking news stories, by highly successful blog posts, and by any number of other legitimate causes. Because of all these possibilities, it is not useful to get too excited about spikes and crashes in traffic reports—unless they are sustained or frequent in occurrence.

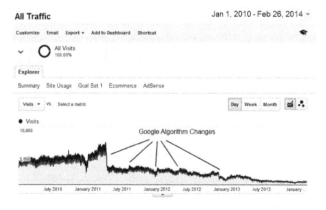

A Website Damaged by Google Algorithm Changes

What is important is to look at the overall trend. Is traffic up, down, or sideways? Downward sloping lines on traffic reports are very concerning, especially if the ROI on the website purchase is far in the future. Sometimes there are good reasons for declining traffic. The website owner may not have added any content to the website for a long time or might not have responded to moves by the competition. While the reason may be valid, you need to be very sure that you are prepared to address the cause of traffic decline effectively.

As an example, many sellers have told me that traffic is in decline because they haven't been writing new articles. I have found that writing new articles rarely affects short-term traffic levels. While it may have been true that the owner hadn't published any new articles recently, it probably wasn't true that this change was the cause of the traffic decline.

A lengthy and stable traffic history is probably the most comforting thing to see in traffic analysis. Steady traffic makes for predictable earnings.

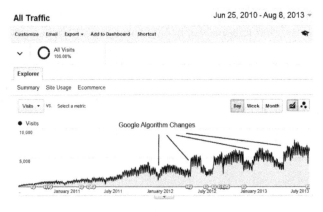

A Website Benefited by Google Algorithm Changes

My content websites receive over 80% of their traffic from Google and a much smaller percentage from Yahoo/Bing and other sources like Facebook. Google is still the dominant player, and that means that anything it does to change the volume of traffic going to one website or another can have a tremendous impact on the fate of your website.

In recent years, it has implemented very significant changes to its search algorithms, resulting in dramatic changes in the amount of traffic websites receive. These algorithm changes have been given names like Penguin, Panda, and Hummingbird. Website owners around the world have bemoaned these changes because their website traffic has crashed or been diverted to unworthy competitors (in their view). Google, for its part, claims that every change results in better and more useful search results for its customers. For the most part, I agree with them.

"Wide diversification is only required when investors do not understand what they are doing."

–Warren Buffett

When a website investor is evaluating traffic, he needs to be aware of the impact of these Google algorithm changes. A stable or growing traffic pattern over the past two years in defiance of four or five major algorithm changes by Google should be seen as a very encouraging sign to the buyer. That means the website has almost certainly been using practices to attract traffic that Google likes or that the traffic is coming from a source other than Google.

I acquired a website that seemed to have benefited from each change that Google made to the algorithms. I interpreted that as an indicator that the site employed very conservative SEO tactics and that its content was very much in alignment with what Google was looking for. The website has continued to receive steady traffic, although it did see a small drop after Google's last algorithm change.

Likewise, websites that have seen precipitous drops in traffic with each Google algorithm change are clearly out of step with Google's best practices for backlink building and content creation. Drops in traffic that occurred in the past may not be a predictor for future drops, however. Much like the stock market "prices in" bad news, Google's changes sometimes take a site down a few notches, while its traffic can remain stable or even grow in the future. Unfortunately, this is a hard thing to determine with certainty, and sites that have had this misfortune must still be considered more risky in your evaluation.

Traffic Changes Unrelated to Google

Sites that show a significant and sustained increase in traffic for no apparent reason should also be considered suspect. Website owners have been known to buy cheap traffic that inflates traffic statistics, but doesn't contribute to sales, in order to boost the perceived value of a website. How can you test this? One way to check is to do searches on keywords that the site seemingly ranks highly for. If Google Analytics shows that a site is getting traffic for "yellow fever treatments" but you search for that phrase on Google and don't seen the website appear on the first few pages, there may be something sinister going on.

If a huge percentage of traffic is coming from "direct" sources, meaning that users are typing in the URL directly, that could be a red flag if there is no good explanation as to why users would be aware of the URL to begin with. Unfortunately, Google and common web browsers have significantly limited the availability of keyword source information, so now it is much more difficult to know which keywords a user was searching for when they arrived at your website. Another impediment is that many searches performed on mobile devices show the traffic as "direct" instead of showing the search engine that the visit actually came from.

If traffic is coming mostly from Facebook, YouTube, or Pinterest, is there any reason it might decline in the future? Find out what the owner has been posting on those pages and make sure you have a plan to continue those postings. Make sure the appropriate Facebook, YouTube, or Pinterest accounts or pages are included in the website sale. If traffic is coming from other sites owned by the seller, get a line in the sales contract that guarantees he will not do anything to disrupt that traffic source. Specifically prohibit the deletion of links, deletion of articles, and any change that would dilute or redirect the traffic.

Paid Traffic

The majority of this section on traffic has addressed free, organic traffic from search engines and other sources. Paid traffic has very different characteristics and needs to be analyzed differently.

Paid traffic is visits to a website as a result of some form of paid advertising. Paid traffic starts when the advertising campaign begins and stops when the campaign ends. Examples of paid traffic sources are ads, videos, commercials, direct mailings, paid guest articles, paid product listings, paid business listings, and radio spots.

Paid traffic is predictable and scalable. Organic traffic is less predictable, and its growth is more difficult to influence. Therefore, paid traffic is less risky than organic traffic. As you will see when we discuss website valuation, sites with predictable traffic are worth more than those with riskier traffic sources.

When you evaluate a site with paid traffic sources, the following points are critical:

- You must ensure those same traffic sources will be available to you after you buy the site. Can the accounts be transferred to your name? Are the sources dependent on some relationship you don't have?

- The seller should demonstrate that the paid traffic is profitable. There should be clear analysis that shows that profit made from customers acquired via a given paid traffic source is greater than the cost of that traffic. *One common mistake is to look at overall profitability of a website and not distinguish profits from paid sources versus free sources of traffic.* The paid sources may not be as profitable as the owner claims them to be.
- The seller must provide all the details of the campaigns that are delivering the customers. This should include all creatives, ad copy, ad network, and private placement contact information, ad network accounts, and if possible, historical campaign information and current ad performance information.

Successful ad campaigns are almost always the result of extensive testing exercises over a long period of time. Therefore, it is important for you, the buyer, to have access to what the seller has tested. You will need to create and test new ads yourself over time, and that process will be much easier if you are building on an historical base of data.

Fine tuning an ad campaign is not as easy as it may seem. Consider the seller of socks. Let's say 5% of the visitors to a webpage buy a pair of socks. That means you will get a sale from one out of twenty visitors. If it costs $.20 per click, you will have spent $4 to attract those visitors. That means the sock order better have ample gross profit to cover the $4 cost of advertising.

The successful, paid advertising operator will have tested and tweaked ad campaigns to reduce the cost per click as much as possible. She will have tuned the sales copy and images on the landing page where the socks are featured to entice visitors to buy at the highest possible conversion rate. She will have tweaked ad copy to attempt to attract real sock buyers—not just sock browsers.

Because getting paid advertising to pay off is a science, it is a valuable asset when it is working well.

Links

Search engines use many indicators to determine how to rank websites in the search results, but the most important indicator is backlinks. Websites that have many other sites linking to them are considered more helpful and popular. If the links come from sites with traffic and authority, search engines consider those links more valuable. Links can also be harmful to a website's ranking if the links come from spammy sites. If Google thinks a website has paid for a link, then the website may well be penalized for violating Google's quality guidelines.

Because links have a major role in influencing search engine rankings and free traffic, it pays to check out the link portfolio. The best place to get a list of links is from the seller's Google WebMaster Tools account in the Links section. Google will let account owners download a list of URLs that are linking to the website. Links from websites you recognize are probably safe. You can easily check out a page that is linking to the website by pasting it into your web browser. Pages that have spammy content are not good link sources. If there are too many of those links, it may mean that the seller has purchased links to try to prop up his website ranking.

If you find too many spammy links or links that the seller has paid for, even if they aren't spammy, the site risks losing traffic and rankings next time Google changes its search algorithm. Algorithm changes happen several times per year and can dramatically affect traffic levels for sites that are dependent on free search traffic.

External tools, like **Ahrefs.com,** provide useful information about the sites linking in, what anchor text they use, what kind of sites they are, and where they are located.

Content

The quality of the pages on a website makes a big difference. Good quality articles, well-described and well-presented products, well-written sales pages, and an original design all add to a website's value.

You will always want to do some cursory checks of the text and images on the site to make sure they weren't copied from somewhere else on the Internet. You can use Copyscape.com, or you can simply copy a paragraph off the page, paste it in Google, and search for the whole block of text. If you find matches, it means someone copied from this website—or this website copied from somewhere else. If the website has thousands of pages, it is fair to ask how all that content was created.

To see whether images are in use elsewhere on the web, you can upload an image file to tineye.com or use the Google "search by image" tool. Assessing whether the image is copyrighted is harder to determine, but if the image is for sale somewhere, that's a bad sign. You should ask the seller to provide receipts of images that were purchased. Ironically, legally purchased images can get you in as much trouble as images you didn't purchase if you have lost the receipt. If an image seller like Getty Images comes after you, it won't matter that you paid for the image if you can't produce proof of purchase.

The Competition

I often find sites that have implemented a great idea that I have never seen before. I get carried away with the idea and forget that what might seem clever and original to me may not be unique at all. That is one reason why it is important to review competitive sites.

Another reason to evaluate the competition is to understand whether the website under consideration is the best in its class and simply needs to stay ahead or whether it is way behind and needs to catch up. It might be very expensive for a site to renovate itself or its product to overtake a well-funded or well-positioned competitor. On the other hand, you might find that a lower-ranking site has great potential because its competitors do not have strong products or a large customer base.

A large number of competitors can indicate that the market or niche is lucrative or broad. Large numbers of competitors are not necessarily something to be afraid of. Entrenched, authoritative, well–funded competitors are more sobering.

Any seller worth his salt can tell you who his competitors are. Simple Google searches, questions in forums, and tools like SEMRush.com can uncover others.

Reasons for Selling

Everyone wants to know why a website is being sold. I certainly do. I want to know whether there is a fundamental flaw in the website that will reduce its future traffic or earnings. I want to know if something has changed in the competitive environment or the customer community that will impact the website. I want to know whether the seller is hopeful about the prospects of the website or worried. I want to know whether the seller has determined that operating the website is a pain in the rear end and can't wait to dump the responsibility on someone else.

Sellers know that buyers want to know these things. Sellers very often write their reasons for selling in the text of the listings. Here is the text I wrote for one of my sales listings:

> I'm a business guy. I am only going to sell if I see some financial advantage in doing so. I manage multiple Internet businesses, including multiple news businesses. The most profitable process I have found is to manage several sites at the same time, sell the ones that are doing well, and then invest effort into making the others do well. So I make most of my money operating the businesses, and I supplement that money occasionally by selling a business.

While I'm on this topic, I sell winners and good performers because I know that I will get a higher price from those kinds of properties. Who wants to buy a site that has a downward-sloping revenue line? So I sell sites with very stable revenue, or growing revenue, in order to get a better price.

Let me add that when most people ask, "Why you are selling?" it is because they think the site has some killer flaw or there has been some event or change in the marketplace that makes the seller want to dump it. Let me just say that there is nothing like that going on here. If the site for some reason doesn't sell, we will keep running it, and it will continue to grow in revenue and profitability. If it does sell, I will take my wife out for a nice dinner.

In point of fact, website buyers don't care at all about the reason the website is being sold—unless the reason includes something negative about the website or about the prospects of the website. I can't tell you how many times I've seen sellers say that the reason for selling the website is that they don't have enough time to invest in it. But in the same listing, they claim that it takes almost no time at all to operate the website. Obviously, both assertions cannot be true. However, these inconsistencies can be useful in determining the veracity of the seller and learning more about the facts of the website.

If the seller provides a legitimate reason for selling the website—or at least one that sounds legitimate to us—then our fear that there is a big, undisclosed problem is reduced. I always ask sellers what the biggest risks are for the future of their websites. If sellers would answer that question honestly, there would never be reason to analyze their reasons for selling. However, because most sellers are afraid to disclose negative information about the website, I ask them why they are selling to uncover more clues about the reality of the situation.

In the end analysis, the "Why are you selling?" question is an integrity check for the seller as much as anything else. Often sellers will offer a more honest answer to this question after they get to know you.

Tip: Asking sellers a large number and wide variety of questions is a good technique for uncovering inconsistencies or missing information about the website.

Dependencies

Some websites have significant dependencies on external websites, suppliers, relationships, accounts, tools, or certifications. You need to be certain that anything the website depends on will be available after the purchase. We will review a few key examples of dependencies.

Suppliers

I once purchased an e-commerce furniture website. The website sold products from six USA-based manufacturers. As agreed, the seller provided me contact information for the six suppliers. All of them required me to apply to be an authorized seller of their goods online. It was a lot of paperwork, and the processing took about eight weeks, but eventually I was approved by all but one supplier. The only problem was that the supplier who did not ultimately approve my application represented about 55% of the sales on this website. Although I signed up with other manufacturers, the website never recovered the sales volume it had before I purchased it.

If the website business model requires that you purchase product at wholesale prices in order to be profitable, you will need to be authorized to sell by the manufacturer or distributor. The fact that the website is already selling that manufacturer's products is helpful, but will not be enough to earn you the right to continue to sell automatically. Some manufacturers require more than others, but many ask for references, bank account information, signatures on MAP agreements (minimum advertised price), and tax IDs. Standards are typically more lax if you are not purchasing inventory on a manufacturer's credit line. If you pay for the product when you order it or put it on your own credit card, then the manufacturer doesn't have to carry any credit risk.

It is a good idea to get the supplier's contact info prior to the website purchase so that you can validate for yourself that there will not be any issues getting signed on as an authorized distributor. *Taking the seller's word for it isn't enough.*

Accounts

Some websites earn their money or receive services from companies that require signups and authorizations. Sometimes sellers are legally able to transfer their accounts over to you as part of the sale, but other times, they are either unable because of the terms and conditions of the provider or because they use the account themselves for other purposes than just the website that is changing hands.

An example is a website I purchased that earned commissions by selling phone, Internet, and television plans from companies like Verizon and AT&T. The former owner had an account with Commission Junction that managed affiliate programs for Verizon and AT&T. I had to first create a new account with Commission Junction. I then had to apply to each telecommunication company to be authorized to place its banner ads and receive sales' commissions from sales of its products. In some cases, approval came easily. In others, there were requirements that I didn't expect. One company refused to give authorization until I had booked a certain number of sales in Commission Junction. It was a catch-22 because I had a new Commission Junction account and needed to be an affiliate before I could make any sales.

Many accounts, like Google Adsense and Google Analytics, are free and very easy to obtain and should not be a concern.

All websites need to live somewhere, and they make their homes on computers called servers. They are located at and managed by web-hosting companies. It is an easy process to sign up for web hosting. There are literally thousands of options to choose from, but the three main strategies (for those who don't already have a preferred web host) should be to open an account with the web-hosting company where the website is currently running, get the seller to transfer her web-hosting account to you, or choose one of the better known companies based on reputation, price, and service.

> "I'm only rich because I know when I'm wrong…I basically have survived by recognizing my mistakes."
> **—George Soros**

If the website has been running fine with limited downtime and the seller vouches for the hosting company, it is sometimes easier to open an account with the same web host because they sometimes transfer websites from account to account for free. Not all hosting companies offer this service, and this recommendation is in the "all-else-being-equal" category.

If the seller doesn't have other websites running under the same hosting account as the site being sold, he may well agree to transfer the account to you and save the effort and risk associated with moving the website to a new hosting account. Some web-hosting companies are happy to do this, while others may require you to fill out a transfer agreement and have it notarized. In some cases, that is more of a hassle than just moving the website to a new account.

It is not within the scope of this chapter to make recommendations for specific hosting companies. A search for "web-hosting comparisons" will bring up a number of websites that compare and contrast web hosts. Be careful because many of those sites don't really help you choose the best provider. They may receive a commission—regardless of which host you choose. For a list of hosting companies and other resources I use, visit **HeckYeah.org/resources**.

Certifications

Some categories of websites may perform functions that are regulated by local law and require certifications from local or national authorities. If the site sells liquor, firearms, or tobacco, for example, you can be assured that a license or maybe more than one license will be required. The need for a license is not necessarily a big deal. However, you need to know what the requirement for obtaining the license will be. If you have to have training or residency in a particular state or a clean arrest record or specific educational requirements, you will want to know those things before you move forward with the website purchase.

Relationships

Many a business is successful because it has a symbiotic relationship with another person, business, or organization. Websites may be created as joint ventures between two completely different businesses. They may receive traffic or support from someone who is not officially on the books. They may have proprietary technology or sophisticated programming that could not easily be supported by anyone besides the creator.

It is quite often the case that a website owner will have all his websites linking to each other. When done wisely, this can increase the search ranking for all of the websites. Any individual site may receive traffic from the others that are linking into it. If one of these websites is sold, part of its ranking and traffic is dependent on the other websites that are still owned by the seller. In this situation, you will want contractual assurances that those links will not be removed or undermined.

Here are some other common situations where there are significant external dependencies:

- A manufacturer or distributor sells off a website that promotes his products.
- A programmer sells off a website that sells his product because he wants to focus on application development but not on sales.
- Customers make recurring payments for a membership. The membership includes access to tools and resources that are hosted and supported by another website owned by the seller.
- A website receives its best leads and customers from the owner's personal network of relationships.
- A website sells services that are delivered by another party.

Contracts: Managing Dependency Risk

When you have identified an important dependency, your first instinct should be to write it into the sales contract. This is important, and we'll talk more about contracts later, but you can do a lot better than just having text in a contract if you keep these three concepts in mind:

1. Incentive. Text in a contract provides some motivation for the seller to do something, but it is not the strongest motivator. Donkeys are motivated more by big carrots than by big sticks. If you can find a reciprocal motivator for the seller to continue doing something or providing something long after the website deal is closed, you will be better off. One motivator, of course, is saying, "Agree to do this, or I won't buy your website." That's okay at a bare minimum, but after the seller gets your money, the incentive goes away. A better statement might be, "If you continue to link to this website, I'll continue to link to yours, and by the way, you are contractually obligated to continue to link to me."

2. Means. Contractually obligating someone to do something that they don't (or won't) have the means or ability to do is an

exercise in futility. A manufacturer isn't going to keep supplying product A if they stop making product A.

3. Reality. In short, wanting something, or twisting someone's arm to agree to something, is not a guarantee that you will get it. The truth is that it is costly and time consuming to enforce a contract legally, and sellers know that. It is much better to reach a mutually beneficial arrangement that is realistic and both parties have an incentive to support. Given a little time, you can often find ways to circumvent dependencies by learning how to do things yourself or finding other sources. But in the short term, key dependencies can make or break your website purchase.

Your Knowledge of the Website's Business

In my "Own the Web" course at **Website-Investors.com**, I emphasize the importance of knowing whether a particular website is a good fit for you personally. Some websites do require considerable, specialized knowledge or experience to sustain and grow profitability. Fortunately for me, most websites don't actually require deep knowledge about any specific sector or niche. But let's consider those that do and what can be done to mitigate the lack of knowledge.

Some websites require technical knowledge to operate because their products are things like software or apps. In order to support the products—and even to sell the products—technical questions must be answered. These problems can be solved in three different ways: outsourcing, automation, and learning.

Outsourcing means hiring a freelancer to provide technical assistance. There is a detailed guide on how to do this in a later chapter. Automation, in this case, might mean putting technical manuals online or writing a sophisticated installation program to cut down on technical installation problems and questions. And learning means biting the bullet, rolling up your sleeves, and learning what you need to learn to answer questions and solve problems yourself.

While the learning curve almost always looks intimidating at the beginning, the 80/20 rule usually comes to your rescue. Most pre-sales and after-sales questions tend to be the same, over and over again. So you may be able to get by with learning the answers to the most common questions and hiring someone as a backup for questions and issues you can't yet handle yourself.

If you are evaluating a website that sells war memorabilia and you are not a connoisseur, it is going to be a challenge to buy inventory at good prices, know what items to buy, answer pre-sales questions, or connect well with your customer community.

For specific niche websites like these, you will almost certainly need a resource with knowledge and passion and availability to help you. Many times these helpers will come in the form of volunteer forum administrators or former or current customers. I have passed up several niche websites that looked like they had excellent prospects because I didn't have enough knowledge of the niche to feel confident that I could be successful.

Sometimes I find myself missing specific marketing skills as well. Websites that require you to write emails or newsletters, websites that require strong skills in pay-per-click campaign management, or websites that require extensive copywriting may stretch your abilities. Again, the three strategies of outsourcing, automating, and learning may suffice to address these challenges, but each strategy has a real cost that needs to be factored into your evaluation of the website's cost and earning potential.

6. Evaluating Future Potential

Sellers love to get you to imagine the future potential of the website they are trying to sell because they know you will pay a lot more if you see great potential. They regularly make claims similar to the following:

- You can easily double the sales of this website by publishing two new articles per week.
- This website is seriously under-monitized. You can make a lot more money by adding new ad networks.
- I'll give you the plan I wrote to grow the website ten fold.
- I have never done any SEO on this website. If you do a little bit of SEO, the site's traffic is sure to take off.
- We only sell a hundred products. There are thousands of other products you can sell to increase revenue.

- I've never tried to make money with this website. It has always just been a hobby for me.
- What the website really needs is some promotion on social media sites, like Facebook and Twitter. Then it will go viral.
- If you buy this website at the buy-it-now price, I'll give you the exact strategies I have used to get one million visitors per month to my other websites.

So you, in turn, may ask the logical question: "If the site has so much potential, why haven't you taken advantage of it?"

And the real answer may be any of the following:

- The seller has already tried everything he can think of to make more money or get more traffic, but he lacks the skills to make it happen.
- The amount of work to make the website grow is more than the seller wants to invest because the probability for success is low.
- The website doesn't actually have much potential to grow.
- The website does have potential and the seller knows that, but for his own reasons, the seller has decided to invest his time and resources in other activities.

Are there websites for sale that have potential for much greater earnings? Absolutely. Every business model and revenue source has "low-hanging fruit," easy things you can change to make more money or attract more customers. Let's look at some classic examples of low-hanging fruit. There are thousands of them.

Advertising Revenue:
1. Use of a low-paying ad network instead of a high-paying one
2. Bad placement of ads on the pages

3. Bad sizing of ads on the pages
4. Ineffective colors or borders
5. Not taking advantage of media ads
6. Not making ad space available to private bidders (relying on contextual ads only)
7. Not taking advantage of responsive ad units for varying device sizes
8. No utilization, or underutilization, of digital product sales or affiliate sales
9. Failure to capture traffic as prospects
10. Overuse of ad space on web real estate
11. Too many distractions

Search Engine Optimization:
1. Bad title tags
2. Missing meta descriptions
3. Limited internal linking
4. Limited incoming backlinks
5. Unmanaged 404 errors
6. Duplicate content
7. Light content
8. No keyword strategy
9. No social network promotion
10. No use of schema markup tags

eCommerce:
1. Product descriptions copied from manufacturer's site
2. Product images copied from manufacturer's site
3. Limited use of sales, discounts, and coupons
4. Unappealing site design
5. Bad user experience

6. Weak guarantee policy
7. Weak customer support
8. No free shipping
9. Weak product selection
10. Lack of product profitability analysis
11. No advertising or ineffective advertising
12. Difficult search and navigation in the website

Affiliate Sales:
1. Low-converting sales copy
2. Visually unappealing
3. Poor product selection
4. Leaks in sales funnel
5. Not taking full advantage of email list
6. Underperforming emails
7. No focus on sales to previous buyers

Leads Sales:
1. Single-lead buyer
2. Untested prices for leads
3. Weak advertising strategy
4. Unexplored sources for leads
5. Leads not qualified

Services:
1. Exceptionally low or exceptionally high prices
2. No evidence of testing different prices
3. No pricing tiers
4. Lack of automation
5. High-priced service providers
6. Low-converting sales copy

7. No pre-sales strategy
8. No advertising
9. No testimonials

When you identify a piece of low-hanging fruit and are confident that making changes to the website could definitely improve its financial performance, then you have concluded that the website has *potential* beyond its current performance. Potential must be quantified. Exactly how much more will the website earn if you increase prices by 20%? Exactly how many more visitors will the website receive if you make much-needed SEO tweaks? How much money will these additional visitors earn you?

Changes you make to improve a website have the potential of helping or harming. Therefore, for each opportunity you identify, you need to estimate a range of possible impact. For example, you might conclude that a change in pricing could yield a 40% improvement in sales as a best-case or a 15% reduction in sales as a worst-case scenario.

Obviously, you will be making a guess here, but you need to quantify the guess so that you can determine whether the hidden potential of the website will increase the price you are willing to pay.

7. Other Countries

As you evaluate websites, it won't be long until you encounter attractive sites based in countries outside your home country. They may have a country-specific extension, like .uk for the United Kingdom, .ca for Canada, .eu for the European Union, or .au for Australia. Or they may have more typical .com, .org info extensions but target customers in a particular country or even a particular city. They may not even be created in a language that you understand. Let's address a few considerations specific to international sites.

Domains

You need to investigate rules and laws associated with specific-country domain extensions. I purchased sites with the .eu TLD and found that owners of .eu domains are required to have residency in a European Union country. Fortunately, I have a partner who resides in the EU. I also learned by chance that domain privacy protection is not available for .eu domains. On several occasions, I have been very interested in buying sites with .au extensions, only to find out that residency in Australia is required for .au domain ownership as well. There are services that will provide a local address that might be sufficient for residency in some situations. The rules change regularly, so the point is that before you buy a website with a country extension, you need to do some quick research on the restrictions. This information is readily available on the Internet.

Websites That Target Specific Countries or Cities

I looked at a website that sold crafts to people in Scotland. It wasn't for me because I don't live there. The website kept a physical inventory and performed self-shipping of the product to customers. Although it might be possible to ship from the USA to Scotland, I quickly rejected the possibility because the cost of shipping and the delays associated with shipping products that distance would not have been good for the business.

An SEO company serviced a big city on the West coast of the USA. The city name was in their URL. They were well established and had a good reputation. After talking to them, I discovered that although they had a solid, local customer base, they almost never met face to face with a customer. The location of the owner was mostly irrelevant as long as one could make periodic phone calls at the right time of day for their customers.

Language Differences

I own several hundred websites in languages I do not speak. I can't even read the URL names for most of these websites. The sites deliver a nice monthly income stream; however, there are some significant limitations. (See the next section on monetization per country as well.) For example, I can't create content myself. I can hire people who know the local language to create content, but even then, I can't check their work. Likewise, I can't read comments or respond to comments. Having said all that, I don't reject websites out of hand just because they are in a different language. There can be some very good deals on internationally based websites. Some markets, like Western Europe, have a strong consumer base, and the percentage of their spending on web-based products and services continues to grow.

International Market Potential

Contextual advertising revenue varies by geographic location because the earnings are based on the amount local advertisers are willing to pay. First-World countries deliver much higher revenue per click than Second- and Third-World countries. It is the location of the user that determines the ads he will see and the amount that is earned per click. A user in the USA will see different ads than a user in Africa in a contextual system. Here are some example earnings per-click averages from a website that has international scope. Don't pay attention to the absolute numbers because this varies greatly depending on the kind of content on your page, but do notice the differences between countries:

Country	Earnings per Click in $
Switzerland	0.49
Martinique	0.48
Sweden	0.45
United Kingdom	0.41
Germany	0.40
USA	0.35
Canada	0.35
Russia	0.24

Italy	0.22
Spain	0.17
Poland	0.14
Haiti	0.12
Ukraine	0.07
India	0.07

Although ad revenue and other kinds of revenue may be lower on a per-transaction basis, there are sometimes large, unexploited markets in different countries. For example, the work-at-home, Internet-marketing niche is filled with competition in the US. In contrast, countries like France and Germany, while having an appetite for those products, have far fewer people selling them.

For the website investor, there are several good strategies here. One of them is to take a site that is performing well in English, in a US market, and translate the site and products into another language. This is less expensive and more easily done than you may expect. I had a fairly extensive real estate website translated into Russian for less than $100. Another strategy is to monitor your analytics for non-English traffic and create a translated copy of pages that are frequented by those visitors. Notice you need to do this based on language, not country.

8. The Fast Flip

I posted on a general forum that I was looking for Google News websites that were for sale. Almost a year later, someone contacted me with a potential site. I ended up buying that one and it performed very well for me. The seller remained in contact after that, and each time he had a site for sale, I was one of the first ones to hear about it.

I was preparing to sell one of my more successful news sites when an email came in offering a newly approved Google News site for sale. The seller wanted $2,500 to start. I offered $1,500, and a few days later, we ended up at $1,800. The value of these sites is that they are syndicated in Google News. The fact that the site was new and had no traffic or earnings history wasn't very relevant.

In its first ten days of operation, the site had generated about $700 in revenue, and $400 of that was profit. Because the ROI was good, my plan was to scale up the number of articles we were publishing.

Meanwhile, the sale of my high-performing site was attracting a lot of attention in the auction. There were at least ten very serious buyers, and six people had already placed bids for more than I had hoped to sell it for to begin with. The auction price was bid up to a level that was making me uncomfortable, so I stopped the auction before the price got too crazy.

I don't often buy sites with the intention of a quick flip, but sometimes the stars just happen to align, and the flip seems like the perfect end to a very good day. This was one of those times. I decided to post my newly acquired site for sale.

Because my auction had just ended with a large pile of bidders anxious to get their hands on a Google News site, the situation was ripe for me to add the second site. I had cultivated relationships with each one of them, so there was a high level of trust. They had placed significant bids, so none of them seemed to be lacking for funds.

I quickly created an auction for the ten-day-old site I had just purchased for $1,800. It got snatched up for $8,000 in less than six hours.

9. Valuation: How Much Should You Pay for a Website?

"It's far better to buy a wonderful company at a fair price than a fair company at a wonderful price."

—Warren Buffett

I determine the price I'm willing to pay for a website business based on three factors:

1. The risk profile. This is a high, medium, low risk assessment that reflects the stability of the business and probable life span.
2. The average monthly net income. Revenue minus expense equals net income. For very seasonal businesses, this needs to be averaged over a full year. For businesses with limited seasonality, an average of the past three to six months is useful.

3. The future potential. Future potential includes every change I
    might make to the website that has the potential to increase
    revenues and profits or reduce risk.

Website valuation is almost always expressed in net income earnings multiples. So if a site nets $1,000 per month and sells for $24,000, it is said to have sold for 24x earnings. If it continues to earn $1,000 per month, then the payback period on the investment is twenty-four months.

Because we speak in terms of multiples, we are often tempted to value sites in terms of multiples as well. We are tempted to think that a site selling for 10x monthly earnings is a three times better deal than a site selling for 30x monthly earnings. That would be true if the sites were exactly the same. But, of course, the risk profile and future potential of the sites could be quite different.

Admittedly, I have aggressively pursued the purchase of sites at low multiples. I've often tried to get my money back in less than a year, and I have succeeded on many occasions. But the truth is that it is increasingly difficult to do this. The vast majority of sites sold at low multiples have a high-risk profile.

The vast majority of sites sold at low multiples have a high-risk profile.

One way to value websites is to decide how soon you want to get your money back and focus on opportunities that meet your target payback period. This is dangerous because it doesn't account for the fundamentals of the website, be they weak or strong.

Assess the Risk Profile

A better way to value websites is to first categorize them by risk profile. The purpose of the chapters on evaluating websites was to identify risks and opportunities. There are an endless supply of risks, but consider these examples to get a feeling for risk categorization:

High Risk	Medium Risk	Low Risk
TRAFFIC Organic search Social media Link schemes Single source	Referring sites Mixed organic/paid Direct traffic Content marketing	Paid Ads (proven campaigns) Email (proven list) Direct mail (proven campaigns) Diverse proven sources
STAFF Highly specialized Not part of deal	Available, unstable situation	Low cost Easy to find, train
PRODUCT Easy to duplicate Single source New/unproven	Semi-difficult to duplicate A few sources Emerging	Difficult to duplicate Multiple sources Proven market
FINANCIALS No formal tracking	Rudimentary tracking	Fully controlled process
BUYER SKILL Inexperienced	Semi-experienced	Experienced, knows niche

As part of your risk assessment, determine how the risk can be mitigated. Often, you as the buyer may bring assets to a website that change the risk profile completely. Consider a buyer who, by virtue of experience, is able to introduce low-risk traffic sources to an existing website. Or, consider a buyer who has deep and specialized knowledge in the business niche of the site she is acquiring. Think of a buyer who already has technical or marketing resources that can be leveraged across the new site to transform a high-risk category to a medium- or low-risk category.

When you make your risk assessment, factor in what you can do to mitigate the risk, but be realistic.

Understand that websites with lower risk will have longer payback periods (and will sell for higher multiples of earnings). Websites with higher risk profiles should have shorter payback periods.

Risk	Earnings Multiple
High	6x – 14x
Medium	12x – 24x
Low	18x – 48x

Risk and time are intimately related because the probability of negative events occurring increases over time. Earnings multiples in the table above are strictly from my own experience and analysis. There is little hard data in this industry. Regardless of the specific multiples, the principle that you should pay less for riskier websites is ironclad.

Does this mean that you should never by a high-risk, low-multiple website? Some would say you should never do it. But the purpose of the table is <u>not</u> to say never. Rather, it is to suggest that you limit your personal investment risk by varying the amount you are willing to invest based on a site's risk profile.

Adjust for Future Potential

If you have uncovered specific untapped treasures in the website, then you will probably be willing to increase the multiple you are willing to pay. As I mentioned earlier, it is important to quantify your estimates for being able to grow revenues or reduce expenses. If you think you can increase the click-through rate on ads by changing their sizes and locations, then you need to extrapolate that potential increase in ad revenues and estimate the change in net earnings. Likewise, if you have devised a way to reduce expenses, you must adjust net earnings by that amount and recalculate the multiple you are willing to pay.

For example, let's say you have determined the website is medium risk and have decided to target a 20x earnings multiple. You have also found ways to increase monthly net income by 30%. You would adjust your earnings multiple upward by 30% and be willing to pay 26x the earnings (20 x 1.3).

What Multiples Are Sites Selling For?

You might ask, the valuation method is fine and good, but what are sites *actually* selling for? What multiple of earnings are sellers willing to sell for in today's market? I might want my money back in twelve months, but are sellers willing to let their sites go for 12x monthly earnings? It depends.

Website business brokers tend to sell sites for higher multiples than marketplaces like Flippa. A quick browse through some brokers' listings will show 36x monthly earnings average asking prices. Other brokers tend to lead with a predictable 24x across the board. Others seem to have more variable pricing, in which you see a range of 12x to 40x. Keep in mind that the average asking price is always higher than average final sale price.

"Price is what you pay; value is what you get. Whether we're talking about socks or stocks, I like buying quality merchandise when it is marked down."

–Warren Buffett

All things considered, website brokers are able to get away with higher prices because they typically offer high-quality properties for sale, having weeded out some of the low-quality ones. They offer higher value properties because it is not worth the cost of their time to list low-priced websites. Some handle only $10,000 websites and above. Others won't touch a website priced less than $50,000 or even $200,000. There is an element of personal selling involved. They foster customer loyalty among a set of investors who can afford to pay and are willing to pay higher prices because they expect to be presented with better-quality opportunities.

All that being said, the trap many brokers fall into is pricing the majority of their listings at the same earnings multiples, with little regard to the risk profile. Granted, there may be some pressure from sellers to go for higher prices, but when I see twenty listings all selling for almost exactly the same multiple, I know the broker doesn't understand or believe that earnings multiples should correlate to site quality and risk profile.

Marketplaces like Flippa sell websites for any price the seller is willing to offer. Earnings multiples vary widely, but it is possible to pick up legitimate sites for as little as 5x multiples of net monthly earnings. Average multiples are more like 10x to 14x. There are plenty of sites on Flippa with numbers in the 18x to 54x range as well.

Your Time

Don't forget to value your personal time investment when you calculate net income. Sometimes buying a website is like buying a job. You might be able to pick up a service-based website for a very low multiple of earnings. Let's say you buy a website that performs resume writing for $15 per page. The website is quite good at delivering customers at that price point, so you can basically earn as much as you have time to write. If it takes you an hour to write each page, then the website becomes an at-home job for you in which you earn $15 per hour. You can still compute a purchase price based on net earnings multiplied by the number of months required to get your money back. But if you value your time at $15 per hour, then net earnings will be zero, and the equation is not very helpful.

Sometimes buying a website is like buying a job. That's okay—if you want a job!

So, in that case, you might consider the purchase in a different way. You might instead view it as a $30,000 per year ($15 x 2,000 hours) job and ask yourself how much you are willing to spend to buy yourself a job writing resumes.

A more typical scenario is that you calculate a website's net earnings **not** taking into account your own time and then ask whether those earnings are worth the time investment. So if net monthly earnings were $300 and you are willing to pay 12x earnings for the site, then you would offer $3,600 for the website. If you also know that it will take about six hours per month to operate the website and you decide to value your time at $25 per hour, then your net monthly earnings will really only be $150. You would then only be willing to pay $1,800 for the website.

I work to drive the highest monthly earning potential, with the least time commitment, out of every website in my portfolio.

If you are valuing your own time at $25 per hour but someone else bidding on the website is valuing their time at $0 per hour, you may be willing to spend only $1,800 for the website, but all things being equal, they would be willing to spend $3,600. Obviously, you would not be the winning buyer.

Smaller time commitments are easier to write off as hobby hours or as a learning experience. Larger time commitments start to cut into career and family obligations. Full-time commitments become careers. I make my living and support my family through the investments I make on the Internet alone. Therefore, I work to drive the highest monthly earning potential, with the least time commitment, out of every website in my portfolio. I do put a rough per-hour value on my time, but I don't use that estimate to alter the amount I will pay for a particular site. Instead, I use that knowledge as a criterion for selecting sites to buy.

Other Valuation Considerations

Assets sometimes come into play when valuing websites. By assets, I mean physical property that will hold much or all of its value over a long period of time. This includes typical business assets, like facilities, automobiles, tools, machines, computer equipment, and inventory. There may also be digital assets, like software, or intangible assets, like patents. However, if a piece of software purchased today with the website won't be able to be sold a year from now, either with or apart from the website, it may not have any current appreciable value.

Only ascribe value to assets if they can be sold quickly.

Only ascribe value to assets if they can be sold quickly. If you can't sell it today or a year from now on its own, you should not consider the value of the asset in the amount you are willing to pay for the website. If there are assets of value, then your valuation equation might look like this:

Asset value + (Earnings Multiple x Net Monthly Earnings) = Offer

You may also buy websites for reasons other than simply monetary ones. Here are some examples of motivating factors:

- Buying a website purely to educate yourself about a niche or a particular business model
- Buying a competitor's website to reduce competition
- Buying a website that is complementary to your own so you can exchange traffic between the two
- Buying a website to create a sales channel for an offline business
- Buying a website to establish credibility
- Buying a website to harvest its tools or systems for use in another business

In such cases, the amount you are willing to pay is much more subjective, but it is still a good practice to attempt to place a dollar value on the benefits you expect to receive and use that as a basis for your offer price.

Other Valuation Methods

Many methods for assessing the value of a website business have been espoused. These include classic capital budgeting methods utilizing Net Present Value, Internal Rate of Return, and the like. They also include methods that attempt to place a unit value on traffic, on an email, or on existing customers.

Unfortunately, these methods rarely prove useful to the website buyer, especially when they are considering sites on the low-end of the spectrum. Many web businesses simply don't have accurate, complete financial information available about the past—much less reliable cash flow projections for the future.

Methods that attempt to put a value on such things, like traffic statistics or email list count, almost always fail because there are dramatic and substantive differences between one email list and another or one visitor to a website and a visitor to a different website.

Market-Driven Comparisons

One approach that does have some theoretical reliability involves analyzing actual sale prices of comparable web properties. Websites with similar characteristics should sell for similar prices—assuming a frictionless market. This process works because, at the end of the day, a site is only worth what a real buyer is willing to pay for it. So, given enough transactions by real buyers, one should be able to deduce going market rates.

This is how it works when you are buying a house. Homes in the same general location with the same number of rooms, square footage, and amenities are considered "comparable." Their sales prices constitute a good rule of thumb for purchase of a similar house.

Website businesses are much more difficult to compare than houses, but sometimes there are enough similarities to make this a valid approach. Use this technique if you are well versed in a particular category, niche, or business model.

There was a time when freshly approved Google News sites where selling in a very tight range from $2,500 to $4,500. I tracked these sales carefully. I owned some of these sites and was qualified to distinguish differences between sites that would affect the value of those sites.

My friend Peter T. Davis is an expert at acquiring and operating forum websites. He can assess the value of forum websites very accurately by comparing them to the many similar sites he has encountered.

To use the market-driven comparison model, list characteristics like revenue source, traffic volume, income level, number of sales transactions, etc. Search for sites that are similar in regard to these characteristics.

Look at the average sales price. If prices vary widely in your sample, you can assume that either you missed an important characteristic or this method is not a good one for the kind of site you are evaluating.

The limitation on this approach is that the kind of information that is required may not be available. This kind of analysis may be performed on Flippa because of the number of transactions and diversity of websites. However, that won't help you much with high-end sites that are typically sold by brokers.

Case Study: Being Conned

It is more than a bit embarrassing to write this chapter about being conned. I had evaluated a website that sold software packages, and I did not win the auction. However, in communication with the seller after the auction, he told me that he had another very similar website and said that he would give me a good price on it. The price sounded good to me, and I'm a big fan of selling software because of its profitability. So I purchased the site and almost immediately started earning money from software sales.

The problem was the domain never got transferred to my name. The seller had disappeared, and I had no way to contact him. He had also failed to deliver some files and support that he had promised. I would like to defend myself, but the truth is that the way I conducted this transaction was indefensible. I made numerous errors, including the following:

- I did not use an escrow process.
- I did not get legitimate contact info from the seller.
- I did not verify that the seller had rights to sell the software (although I had asked the seller about that).

- I accepted the seller's excuse that there was a problem in transferring the domain and that he would resolve it the next day.
- The seller had offered to let me continue to use his web host. I took him up on the offer.

After I understood that I had been ripped off and was not in control of the domain, I immediately purchased another similar domain name and published all the website content and products for sale under the new domain. I continued to operate the website I had purchased for another three months. At that time, the seller removed my access to the web-hosting account and replaced the website with his own website so that sales began to flow to him instead of me.

The end of this story may not be as bad as what you think. If the majority of traffic and sales had come from search engines, this would have ended badly. The new domain I had purchased as a backup for the one that had been stolen from me would have required a long time to begin generating traffic on its own.

As luck would have it, and I do mean luck, because I certainly didn't plan it this way, the primary traffic source was paid advertising on HotScripts.com. I was able to redirect traffic from Hot Scripts to the new domain name, and the setback in sales turned out to be very minor.

Although no one ever accused me of copyright infringement, I discovered that I could not legitimately sell some of the software products on the website. I sold the website and provided full disclosure about the software license situation to the buyer, who did not seem too concerned about it. Overall, I tripled my investment in about five months.

But that wasn't the only time it happened.

I purchased a Google News site from a guy on Flippa. The transaction went smoothly; the domain and website were transferred, and I began to operate the site. Google News sites are typically valued on the basis of their inclusion in Google News—not on their historical performance. However, after the first few weeks of publishing articles, this website was not performing nearly as well as my other Google News sites. I contacted the seller, and he agreed to refund three fourths of the payment I had made and take the website back. Over the course of a month, I contacted the seller repeatedly, but he never returned the money, and I never heard from him again.

While this was not a scam in the sense that the seller purposely tried to defraud me, I still ended up losing my entire investment. While I was waiting for the seller to refund my money, I stopped publishing articles on the website. Google News apparently took that as a sign that I was not a serious news publisher and removed the website from the Google News index. This action made the site worthless.

10. The Auction and Negotiation

I am writing this chapter after sitting on both sides of the negotiation table for many website transactions. There are a few obvious—and a few not so obvious—strategies for closing a deal and paying the sum you want to pay.

Ingratiation

The first strategy I'll discuss is ingratiation, and it is all about relationship. There is a dysfunctional mindset in monetary transactions that the person who is forking over the dough has a right to be a jerk because he is the customer in this particular exchange. This is not a new idea to anyone who has ever sold something. The person doing the selling is expected to maintain a sense of professionalism at all times—even in the face of hostile behavior from customers. Buyers feel righteous justification in making presumptuous demands and communicating them in a less-than-professional way.

As a buyer, this cultural paradigm can be used to your advantage.

From the first communication with the seller, be nicer and more professional than any other potential buyer. You want the seller to be cheering for you in the auction and hoping that you will be the winner. Is this just about warm, fuzzy feelings? Not at all. I have had sellers stop the auction and award the sale to me because they didn't like the people I was bidding against. Sellers can certainly try to manipulate you with their language, but I've had several sellers tell me early in the auction process, sincerely, I believe, that they hoped I would win. That level of relationship is self-fulfilling.

"Persist—don't take no for an answer. If you're happy to sit at your desk and not take any risk, you'll be sitting at your desk for the next twenty years."

—David Rubenstein

Make yourself known as a person, not just an anonymous buyer. Early in the communication process, explain who you are and why you want to buy the website. Besides telling a seller why his website would be a good fit for me, I tell him about myself. I say where I'm from; tell him I make a living owning Internet sites; and I explain that this is how I support my wife, four kids (two of whom are in college, another is special needs), and a fat dog. I tell him my wife is always looking over my shoulder so I don't make crazy decisions. In summary, I am vulnerable with the seller because I want him to be vulnerable with me.

Once I become a person, not just a buyer, several things happen. If the seller was planning on cheating me, he now thinks twice because there is a little bit of humanity in almost everyone. He feels more of an obligation to treat me like a person, rather than like an anonymous email address. He is more thorough in his answers to my questions, more honest and more helpful. He offers information that I didn't even ask for. He ends up investing time and effort in our relationship, and he loses something if I don't win the auction. Amazingly, he even begins to care whether I like him.

Besides being personal, I am also identifiable. In my first message, email, or phone call, I use my full name and very often provide a phone number, email address, or Skype account where I can be reached. In my marketplace profile, I provide links to my Facebook and LinkedIn accounts. I want the seller to know I have nothing to hide. This information also gives him assurance that he will be able to find me at any time in the future. This single step differentiates me from 95% of the people who are interested in buying the site.

What I get by ingratiating myself to the seller is obvious: better information about the website; a potentially better price; much better post-sale support; a new colleague in the Internet business (regardless of whether I end up buying the site or not); and glowing feedback on my Flippa profile if the sale goes through.

The seller gets a chance to sell to someone they like, a potentially higher price if they reciprocate in kind, and an easy person to work with. As a seller, I've had a few really difficult buyers, and I've had some who are the salt of the earth. I go out of my way to do business with the good ones, and there are many times I would have taken 10-15% less to be able to deal with a more reasonable person after the sale. Experienced sellers understand this and seek out buyers they like and believe are trustworthy.

To recap:

1. Be THE nicest buyer.
2. Be personal.
3. Be identifiable; don't disguise your identity.

Some readers will be skeptical about the strategy of ingratiation and may be uncomfortable to think of sharing any identity or personal information with an unknown seller. Clearly, you never want to be naïve or expose yourself to the threat of identity theft. However, providing basic contact information and sharing a little about yourself won't put you at risk. Regardless of the amount of information that you share, do it in the most gracious way possible.

Tip: Jesus said, "Do unto others as you would have them do unto you" (Luke 6:31). This is my basis for using the principle of ingratiation as a buyer. I also let this mindset inform every other business relationship I engage.

The Auction

Flippa and some other marketplaces offer <u>private</u> and <u>public</u> listing formats. Public-style listings are sold via auction. Private-style listings are sold via sealed bid and awarded at the discretion of the seller.

Public auctions have a fixed initial duration of anywhere from a couple of days to thirty days or more. In the hopes of attracting bids, sellers want as many people as possible to read their auction listing. There are three important numbers in each listing:

1. Minimum bid—the lowest amount anyone may bid
2. Reserve price—the lowest amount the site will sell for
3. Buy-it-now price—a price, which if bid, will immediately end the auction

The minimum bid may be below the reserve price. Sellers often like to set the minimum bid at $1 to attract as many bids as possible. If a bid is placed below the reserve price, the seller is not obligated to sell at that bid. The seller must sell at any bid offered at or above the reserve price.

It has become a common practice for sellers of low-end websites to set the reserve price at $1 and the minimum bid at $1. In this scenario, the seller knows that they might have to sell the site for $1 if only one bid is placed. However, the strategy is used to collect as many bids as possible. People are more likely to bid because each bid could potentially win the auction. The more bids that are made, the more visibility an auction has. On Flippa, there is a "Most Active" auctions page. The more bids an auction receives, the higher the auction moves on the most-active list. The higher on the list, the more people see the auction and go check it out.

Savvy buyers understand this strategy and hold most, or all, of their bids until the end of the auction. Buyers do not want to create more competition for themselves by bidding early and often in an auction, thus giving it more visibility.

There are two exceptions I make to the rule of not bidding before the end of the auction:

- If I want to let a seller know that I am a serious buyer, I place a significant bid (but usually one that is below the reserve price).
- If a seller has created a no-reserve auction to attract a lot of bids, then I want to limit the number of bids, to limit visibility. In this case, I sometimes bid a high amount early in the auction, an amount below what the website is worth, but high enough to discourage frivolous bids.

Flippa has implemented an auto-bidding feature that allows you to enter the highest amount you are willing to pay for a website, and then Flippa automatically bids on your behalf in small increments up to your limit price. If you were willing to pay no more than $1,000, for example, you would enter that as your maximum bid. If another bidder bid $100, the Flippa system would automatically add a minimum increment to the $100 and bid that amount for you. The automated bidding would continue until the auction ended with your bid as the winner or until the competition bid you up to $1,000. This system is convenient if you don't have time to watch the auction closely and place individual bids, but it creates a higher number of bids in total and works in favor of the seller, who wants his auction to appear more active.

Reserve Prices

Because reserve prices are not usually revealed in sales listings, you won't know the minimum price the seller is willing to accept unless you ask. This is something you want to know early in the auction because you don't want to waste time on auctions that are way out of your price range. Ask what the reserve price is. If you don't get an answer, ask the question a different way: "Approximately how much are you hoping to get for this?" Or, try, "How would you compute the value of this website?" If you can't get a direct answer, the site may still be appealing enough for you to continue evaluating the site and hang around until the end. However, unrealistic price expectations are very common, and if the seller is reluctant to share the reserve price, that's an indication the price might be out of bounds.

Seller's Reputation

If you are bidding on Flippa or another marketplace that collects information about buyers and sellers, it is a very useful first step to check out an individual's profile. You can see several pieces of key information:

- Is the seller an active buyer and seller?
- What websites has he sold in the past and at what price levels?
- What websites has he purchased in the past and at what price levels?

- What feedback has he received from prior transactions as buyer or seller?
- What percentage of his listings were sold?
- Does the marketplace have any recorded disputes related to the seller? Did he win or lose the dispute?
- Has the seller supplied a Facebook, Google +, or LinkedIn account?
- What country is the seller from?

All of these bits of information give you insight into the trustworthiness of the seller. You may also learn what niches and business models he specializes in. You may choose to "follow" a particular seller so that you receive notifications each time the seller offers a new website for sale.

"You don't need to be a rocket scientist. Investing is not a game where the guy with the 160 IQ beats the guy with 130 IQ."

–Warren Buffett

I like to read past sales listings written by the seller to see if he is really providing unique and specific information about each website he sells or if he is just writing boilerplate sales text. I read the comments written by prospective buyers to get a sense for whether the seller is generally trusted or raises suspicion.

If the seller's true identity and location seem relevant to me, I don't hesitate to ask him about it directly. It is always prudent to obtain enough information about the seller that you can track him or her down should something go amiss during the transaction. For large purchases, it is even worthwhile to do a background check on the seller.

Communication

Most auction systems have public comment and private messaging capabilities. I generally avoid making public comments because I don't want to show my interest publically and thereby attract more buyers as competitors. My personal introduction and initial salvo of questions is sent via private message. I include my full name and contact information so that the seller will have confidence early on that I am a serious buyer.

As the auction progresses and I get more serious about bidding or buying, I naturally have more questions. Often the answers are complex and need more explanation than is comfortable in an email or private message. I suggest having a conversation over the phone or on Skype. Skype calls, TeamViewer, or other chat systems are effective because the seller can share his screen and show you the website while answering your questions. It's a good idea to record your own screen while he shares his so that you can review the information later on. You will want him to walk you through proof of sales, proof of traffic, and anything that the public can't access (like behind the scenes administrative panels and tracking systems).

Access to information you have never seen before will generate more questions and produce more answers, helping you make a better decision. You will also be able to assess how knowledgeable and helpful the seller will be after the auction.

Non-disclosure Agreements

Some sellers will require bidders to sign NDAs to protect proprietary information about the website or business being sold. This is a legitimate request under normal circumstances, not something you should be afraid to sign. I say normal circumstances because there may be situations where you are evaluating a competitor's website or encounter a situation where you might be exposed to information that would make it uncomfortable for you to conceal. It is unwise and unethical to violate such agreements once signed.

Non-compete Agreements

As a buyer, you will often come across websites that are the brainchild of the seller and you will sense that the seller could easily become your competitor after you buy the site. It is common and appropriate to ask the seller if they are willing to sign a non-compete agreement. Non-compete agreements can contain any provisions you like, but these documents commonly specify the following:

- That the seller not participate in a particular niche or market for a fixed period of time
- That the seller not sell particular kinds or models of products for a fixed period of time
- That the seller not perform work for a competitor in the same business arena for a fixed period of time

It is clearly to the buyer's advantage to have broad language so that the seller can't find ways to compete by finding loopholes in the agreement. Sellers may want to limit the effective period of the agreement. Sellers also may flatly refuse to sign a non-compete and that may or may not be a show-stopper. In broad markets where the seller doesn't have a particularly compelling or proprietary advantage, the absence of a non-compete may not be a big deal. Conversely, if the website is a 'one trick pony' and the market is small, competing with the seller might be a death knell.

Getting Creative

Some deals are made when you have the flexibility to offer something other buyers can't or didn't think of. For example, one website sale would have resulted in dead office space, an expense the seller would be stuck with. The buyer offered to rent the space in exchange for a reduced price.

Likewise, I once purchased a large network of sites that would have proved difficult to migrate to a new web host server. The seller couldn't transfer the whole server to me because there were a number of other websites residing on the same server. In the end, I agreed to buy the additional sites at a very small additional cost, and the seller was able avoid all the work involved with migrating the websites to another server.

Case Study: Pure Mountain Pee Pee

I look at hundreds of websites and buy just a few. I was intrigued when I saw a site with very low traffic and a very high conversion rate. Almost everyone who visited the site was making a purchase. Looking at the traffic statistics, it was unclear which search terms were leading people to the website. But however they got there, they must have known exactly what they were looking for because sales were consistent over a good number of months.

The strange thing was that the product description wasn't easy to find on the website. The product was shipped in unmarked, brown paper packaging to any address in the USA. It was laboratory processed and certified to be free of drugs, disease, and pollutants.

They were selling urine. And the customers were people who wanted a clean urine sample to use to pass drug tests.

Needless to say, I passed on that one.

---

11. The Handoff

A fter there is agreement on price, there is a series of tasks that need to happen to move the website from seller to buyer. These chores range from few and simple to many and complex.

Sales Contracts

Contracts are not just for suing people. The most important function of a contract, of any kind, is force the parties to think through the transaction they are entering into and communicate all the details to each other on paper. It clarifies roles and responsibilities and reduces future ambiguities in the relationship. The second most important function is to provide incentive to both parties to do what each agreed to do. There is something about having an agreement on paper, with signatures, that increases the weightiness of a promise—irrespective of whether a contract is legally enforced. The third purpose is, of course, the ability to obtain restitution if one of the parties violates the contract and there is no other mechanism to force them to fulfill their obligations.

With all that said, most transactions in life don't require contracts. We buy things every day with no contract in place. Websites are the same story. The majority of small website transactions do not require a sales contract. One party provides the money; the other party hands over the website, and everybody is (theoretically) happy. The transaction is consummated when they buyer gets everything he purchased and the seller is paid.

However, larger websites and those with assets, accounts, external dependencies, promises of significant post-sale support, high-risk transitions, or high-dollar sales prices really need a sales contract to accomplish the three functions explained above. Brokers, and even Flippa, offer sales contract templates and assistance in filling them out. Details will vary considerably, but generally speaking, the following aspects of the transaction will be addressed:

- The assets to be transferred, detailing what is included and what is not included
- The purchase price
- The effective date of the agreement and how sales, expenses, and debts are treated before and after the agreement
- Assurance that the seller is the rightful owner of the assets
- Responsibilities of the seller, particularly in the transition period and post-sale
- Responsibilities of the buyer
- What happens in the time period before the agreement closes (i.e., the seller needs to keep operating the website in good faith)
- How to handle dependencies like third-party agreements

Non-compete Agreements

Executing a non-compete agreement can be a condition in the sales contract. Non-competes should be signed prior to the transfer of money.

Paying for the Website

Most website purchases should proceed through an escrow service. See the next section for much more detail about how escrow works.

Escrow.com accepts wire transfers, credit cards, PayPal, and checks or money orders, but not for every transaction. There are detailed restrictions related to all payment types—except wire transfers.

For transactions in which you choose not to use escrow, you will need to agree on payment type with the seller. There will be risk to one party or the other because either you have to pay before you get the website, or the seller has to hand over the website before he gets paid. These risks can be mitigated somewhat by breaking the transaction into pieces. For example, you might pay 33% in one payment, which spurs the seller to transfer only the domain to your name. Then, you might agree to pay another 33% for another portion of the site and so on. You may be protected legally with a sales contract without using an escrow process, but enforcing contracts in court is expensive and time consuming.

I have used PayPal for low-end site purchases a number of times. I usually do it when I have some relationship with the seller or have reason to believe there is not a significant risk.

Escrow

All but the tiniest of transactions should use an escrow process to protect buyer and seller. Escrow companies manage the sales transaction as follows:

- Transaction initiated by buyer or seller
- All agreed assets, services, and dependencies are listed in the transaction
- Length of inspection period is documented in the transaction
- Buyer and seller agree to the content of the transaction
- Buyer sends money to the escrow company
- Escrow notifies seller that funds have been received
- Seller performs physical transfer of assets and other agreed items to buyer
- Buyer notifies escrow that the goods have been received
- Inspection period begins
- Buyer inspects all components of the transaction
- Inspection period expires or buyer signals satisfaction with the received goods
- Escrow releases funds to seller

In a properly performed escrow transaction, the seller is protected because the buyer's payment is secured before the seller gives the website to the buyer. The buyer is protected because he can make sure he has received everything before his money is released to the seller. Escrow. com provides this service specifically for websites. They provide excellent customer service along the way, and the small fee is well worth the protection provided.

The alternative to using an escrow service, as I mention above, is to break the assets up into small sections and transfer money from the buyer to the seller in pieces as each section of the website is transferred. The total amount of risk is reduced; however, each section of the transaction still carries risk. It is much better to go with an escrow process.

Executing a sales contract does not exclude using an escrow service. In fact, the two work quite well together as most of the provisions in the contract fit nicely into the content of the escrow transaction. Some items in the contract, like provision of post-sale support by the seller, would naturally not be supported by the short escrow inspection period and would have to be enforced by contract.

Tip: The duration of the inspection period is negotiable. Make sure the inspection period is long enough to provide a reasonable sample of traffic and sales. If the website's sales or traffic are sporadic, then you may not be able to measure the website's performance adequately during the inspection period.

Physical Transfer of the Website

The responsibility for transferring the website from seller to buyer is agreed upon during the auction and most often falls on the seller. Let's discuss the components that have to be transferred in most transactions.

The Domain

Domains are managed globally by an organization called the Internet Assigned Numbers Authority (IANA). The management of specific groupings of domain names is delegated to other organizations called domain registries. All domains are purchased from domain registries that track the individual and corporate ownership of domain names.

When a domain changes hands, the owner name and contact information change. The domain registrar may or may not change, depending on the preference of the buyer. Changing domain ownership is usually a free transaction that is initiated by the current owner of the domain; the seller simply fills out a form with the current domain registrar. These transactions happen thousands of times per day. The typical transaction looks like this:

- The seller tells the buyer that the domain is registered at GoDaddy.com.

- The buyer opens a free account at GoDaddy.com and sends the seller his account information.
- The seller then asks GoDaddy to transfer the domain from the seller's account to the buyer's account.

The Web Host

Websites live on servers that are owned and managed by web-hosting companies. There are two primary strategies for transferring a website from one owner to another. One is to move all the files and databases of the website from the old to the new server. The other is to transfer the web-hosting account in its entirety from the seller to the buyer.

In the first scenario, which is by far the most common, you will need to sign-up for a web-hosting account. There are many to choose from, but some of the biggest names are Host Gator, Yahoo, GoDaddy, Bluehost, iPower, and IX Webhosting. The biggest aren't necessarily the best, so do some quick research online before selecting one. My personal recommendations are listed at **HeckYeah.org/resources**.

If the website's current web-hosting company is providing good service and good uptimes for the website, you might consider opening an account with them. In some cases, this may make transferring the website a little easier.

If the seller is willing to transfer his web-hosting account to your name, then it will save the effort and possible disruption of moving the website to a new server. However, sometimes a seller will not be willing to give you the account because he has other websites on the server that are not part of the deal. One wrinkle in handing over web-hosting accounts is that many web-hosting companies—if not all of the legitimate ones—require a notarized document to officially recognize the new owner. Simply changing the name, password, and payment information on the account is not enough to satisfy their terms of service.

Moving the Website Content

The most common scenario is the physical move of the website from the seller's server to the buyer's server. This is a technical task, and although it is not overly complex, it is best performed by someone who has done it before and is familiar with all the components of the website that need to be moved. The buyer must first sign up for a web-hosting account, which will provide a server that is to be the future home of the website. Keep in mind that visitors to your website won't know or care where the website is hosted. They should not be able to tell that the website moved from a server in Chicago to one in Dallas—unless, of course, the one in Dallas is much slower or faster.

Tasks in the move include the following:

- Copying all the website files, including documents and images
- Copying the database of the website
- Copying email files associated with the website and setting up those email accounts (The buyer will need to have access to the new email login info and begin checking those emails.)
- Changing the name servers to point at the new server
- Setting up any batch jobs to run on the new server that were running on the old server

While these steps may sound complex, for small- to medium-size websites, all these tasks can often be completed in less than an hour.

Lots of Accounts

As websites grow, they tend to accumulate accounts that need to be transferred to the new owner when the site is sold. These include social networking accounts, like Facebook, Twitter, Instagram, Pintrest, and Google+; advertising networks like Adsense or BuySellAds; analytics like Google Analytics or Clicky; merchant accounts like PayPal or Skrill;

affiliate accounts like Clickbank or JVZoo; email accounts like Aweber or MailChimp; and countless others.

Some of these accounts, like Facebook pages, are easy to transfer. It's just a matter of changing the admin from one Facebook user to another. Others simply require handing over the user ID and password. Still others, like Adsense, can't be transferred at all, and the new owner is forced to open his own account, which may require approval. It is important to have a list of all the accounts and a plan for their transfer— lest some of them fall through the cracks.

The Inspection Period

After you have received everything the seller promised to provide, the escrow inspection period begins. At this point, you have already evaluated the business aspects of the website. You decided you wanted it; you won the auction; and you sent payment that is sitting in escrow. You and the seller have done a lot of work to get to this point, and both of you are hoping that there won't be any glitches that derail the transaction.

The dual goals of the inspection period are to:

- Verify that you received everything you paid for
- Verify that everything you received is substantially as advertised

The first goal should be relatively easy to achieve. It's a good practice to make a list of all the things you expected to receive as part of the transaction and simply go down through the list checking things off. I list below a sampling of things that may be included:

- The domain(s)
- The website(s)
- Accounts (social, advertising, affiliate, analytics, etc.)

- Supplier introductions and contact info
- Employee and freelancer introductions and contact info
- Documentation (guides, manuals, instructions)
- Digital products (eBooks, videos, courses)
- User IDs/passwords to everything
- Support from the seller (This will probably not be limited to the inspection period.)
- Physical inventory
- Physical equipment

Make sure to capture promises made by the seller in your pre-sale discussions, as well as documenting every item that was listed in the original listing, including bonuses and buy-it-now incentives.

The second goal of making sure that everything you received is substantially as advertised is slightly more subjective and time consuming. You will want to go down the list of deliverables again, this time looking at quantities and quality. But, of course, the critical metrics are sales and traffic. If those two things are as you expected, chances are you are home free. If sales or traffic are off, you and the seller will immediately embark on a search for the reasons and causes. If the reasons aren't good enough, the deal will go south.

Most websites are subject to seasonality of some kind. Swimsuits sell in the summer. Fewer homes are purchased during the winter. School calendars and holidays significantly influence traffic and sales. Additionally, most websites have traffic patterns related to the day of the week or time of the month. Many of my websites have less traffic on the weekends and have the most traffic on Mondays. You will need to take seasonality and traffic patterns into account as you judge the sales and traffic volume during the inspection period.

If you have set your inspection period long enough, then you should have a good idea as to whether the numbers you are seeing are in keeping with your expectations and in alignment with historical performance. Longer inspection periods benefit the buyer. Negotiate the inspection period length before you reach a final agreement on price. While very simple sites can be inspected in as little as three days, most inspection periods should run a minimum of a week.

Websites with sporadic sales patterns are harder to assess. I own a site that sells software. Sometimes there are no sales for two weeks, and sometimes there are two or three sales on the same day. When I purchased the site, there were no sales at all during the seven-day inspection period. In fact, there were no sales for the first three weeks I owned the site, and I was getting very worried. The pattern broke after three weeks, and there were a few big sales that made up for the slow period.

Because there were no sales during the inspection period, I was looking very closely at traffic. The number of visitors to the site seemed to be completely normal and consistent with historical numbers. The sources of the traffic also looked legitimate. Although I was a little bit concerned, I went forward with the purchase, and it turned out to be a good decision.

The big advantage you have during the inspection period is full access to all the statistics. Pre-sale, you were most likely limited to reading reports that were snapshots in time. Post-sale, you have access to the analytics system so you can drill down into the numbers as far as you like and study these details: which devices your customers are using to access your site; how long they are spending on each page; how many pages they look at before getting bored and leaving; whether your traffic is coming from Bing, Facebook, or Google; and which ones are trending up and down.

On the monetary side, you will be able to see not only how many people are clicking on ads, but you can also see which website page they are on when they click. You'll be able to find out which size ads are performing best and which placement on the page is attracting the most clicks. You'll know specifically who is buying your products, where they are from, and at which price level they are buying. You will be able to spend as much or as little time as you like sifting through all this detail to assess whether everything is kosher or whether you've been wasting your time.

If you decide to back out of the transaction, you will have a lot more basis for doing so if sales and traffic numbers are different than those the seller had presented. However, there may be other material differences that justify canceling the deal as well, such as the following:

- A key person, like the former writer for the site, did not transfer over as promised.
- The website doesn't function correctly, and the seller can't or won't fix it.
- The seller fails to provide a key dependency for the business as promised, like supplier contact information or access to digital assets.
- The seller didn't continue to operate the business responsibly in the interim period before you take control.

If you have a signed contract of sale in place, it will likely cover these possibilities, giving you the legal grounds to back out.

Pulling the Trigger

Once you are satisfied that you've received everything and it is performing as expected, you notify escrow that you have accepted the website. Escrow releases the funds to the seller, and the website is officially yours.

In my experience, sellers are feeling quite comfortable at this point in the process. They have received the money and have relieved themselves of the responsibility of operating the website. If the buyer has managed the transaction correctly, he now has a good working relationship with the seller, and the seller is ready to provide his best advice for taking the website to the next level.

Case Study: The Furniture Business

I will spare you the details of how I found and acquired a furniture eCommerce site and will instead focus on what I learned after I became the happy owner. The website sold home furnishings and furniture. There were over 3,000 products, from tiny items like bookends to large items like sofas and bedroom suites. It was a simple business model. People found our site by searching the web for a piece of furniture. They purchased items on our site. We placed an order with the manufacturer, and the manufacturer shipped the order to the customer. I was the middleman, and revenue came from adding a markup to the amount we paid the manufacturer and shipping company.

There were seven manufacturers, and I had to apply to each one separately to sell their products—even though the website I bought had already been selling the products for some time. The manufacturer relationship is with the owner of the website, not with the website itself. The majority of the manufacturers required, or desired, to do business with a registered business, not simply an individual with sole-proprietor status, so I registered an LLC.

One of the key suppliers, who represented more than half of the site's revenue, decided to evaluate its Internet channels and did not process my application for two months. During that time, I could not sell its products. At the end of the two months, the manufacturer decided that my website did not sell enough of its product, so it rejected the application. This was the first of several fatal blows taken by the site. I worked hard to sign up other suppliers and was successful with two, but they did not make up for the lost sales or traffic generated by the original supplier.

At that time, Google featured eCommerce products like ours in Google Shopping for free. You simply had to set up an account and provide Google with product information and your products showed up alongside those from Sears, Walmart, Amazon, and the other big boys on the Shopping page. Apparently, those were the good old days. Shortly after I bought the furniture business, Google began to transition to a paid-only program. To have products highlighted in Google Shopping, you now had to do it through Google Adwords and pay for the privilege. This was a traffic killer. I tried to go the paid traffic route, but it didn't work out. Managing paid advertising campaigns profitably for a website with thousands of products requires a great deal of skill and diligence. I was short on the skill and definitely lacked the motivation.

The site did sell furniture, despite those setbacks. But furniture is heavy, making it costly to ship. Furniture sometimes breaks in transit, requiring returns. Furniture doesn't look the same on websites as it does in your living room. You can't sit on a couch on the website. These factors also result in returns. Customers who pay for expensive items expect superior service. All of these obstacles are costly financially. They are also time-consuming.

Managing thousands of products on a website requires good tools, patience, and attention to detail. New products need to be added, and manufacturers provide item information in different formats. Existing products are sometimes discontinued. Costs of products change, and competitors change their prices. That means the eCommerce site manager needs to consistently update pricing to avoid loss of profit and to keep up with the competition. People buy things that are on sale. Whether online or offline, retail sales requires vigilant marketing, making liberal use of tools like coupons, sales, incentives, advertising, and product showcasing on websites.

The good news is that profit margins were good and most of the products were high-ticket items.

After about six months, I had recouped about 30% of the initial investment, and I let the website fade into oblivion. There was too much work, too little sales, and too much stress to keep it going. My other website purchases were performing well, so I had even less incentive to work to turn this one around.

Goal: low effort or no effort	Result: high effort
There was a ton of work involved in updating product information, adding new products, and shepherding orders through to completion.	
Goal: low risk	**Result: high risk**
Lost traffic from Google policy changes. Lost suppliers from their own policy changes.	
Goal: long life	**Result: short life**
I let it die early. With a great deal of effort, the business would probably be around to this day. The business model is not short-lived, but my patience was.	
Goal: Google resistant	**Result: sensitive to Google**
Google policy changes greatly reduced traffic levels.	

Goal: short payback period	Result: lost money
Recouped only 30% of the initial investment.	
Goal: high quality service	Result: high quality
The products were good, quality products, and we provided professional, personalized service.	

12. It's Mine; Now What?

The moment of truth has arrived. You have a new baby, and like a parent, you are very excited. At the same time, you are wondering what in the world you have gotten yourself into. Thousands of books have been written on operating a website from technical, marketing, content, sales, and operational perspectives. In fact, there is too much information available, and it can feel overwhelming as you begin. But do not despair; this chapter will home in on the most crucial things to focus on out of the gate.

Getting Help

Almost everyone needs a little external help at some point along the way. The seller is always the first and best resource, but he is by no means the only source of help. The good news is that help is actually incredibly easy to find, and it doesn't have to be expensive. The not-so-secret world of freelancing is at your fingertips. There is someone willing to do almost any conceivable project for you. In fact, there are a lot of someones who will compete for your odd job. Freelancer.com recently announced its one-millionth freelancer. Elance.com, Odesk.com, and many others are online marketplaces, matching those who have skills for sale and those who need something done for a good price.

As the new owner of a website, you may need content created, technical problems fixed, marketing plans written, traffic boosted, conversions increased, customer support help, or faster webpage response times. You might need one-time help, part-time help, or full-time help. All of these are available in freelancer marketplaces. Just create an account, validate your payment details, and you are good to go.

I start by searching project listings and looking for projects that are similar to my needs. This gives me examples to follow as I create my own project. I read the skill requirements others asked for and the detailed project descriptions given to help me think through my own requirements. Then I simply type up a quick project description, pick from a list of skills, choose the least expensive option for posting my listing, and click go. Some marketplaces make money by charging the freelancer a percentage fee; others charge the hiring party, and some have fees for both. Buying upgrades to promote your listing is rarely necessary.

Unless you are looking for a very specific, narrow skillset, you are likely to get plenty of proposals to choose from. The freelancer marketplace is truly global, and this will be evident in the varying levels of English skills exhibited by those who apply for your job. But English isn't the only skill that will vary; the core professional skills will too.

To minimize the time you spend wading through proposals, look first at those who have a history of successful projects. Browse the feedback received and verify that there is positive feedback on projects where the freelancer has done work similar to your own. Tightwad that

I am, I give the low-priced bids a hard look first. The combination of positive feedback history and low price is often a winner for me. The other important indicator I look at is whether a candidate has demonstrated that they understand what I want. They do this (or don't do this) by what they write in their proposals. If the freelancer has listed your key requirements and specified how he will accomplish them, he has placed himself above 95% of the field. I have had several freelancers create a demo, do a sample task, or write a sample article for me while I'm deciding whom to pick.

I have found some wonderful freelancers in marketplaces over the years; a few of whom have become loyal employees and friends. It is true that there are some bad eggs, and your first choice may not be as skilled or responsible as you would have liked, but I have never failed to find excellent help at a good price with a little persistence.

Tips For Managing Freelancers

Payment. You pay the marketplace where you located the freelancer, and that site pays the freelancer.

Project completion. Marketplaces usually have the ability to set up milestones within projects. A freelancer may ask you to separate payment into multiple milestones so that she may be compensated as each task is completed. Freelancers may also request that you pre-fund the milestones. This tells the freelancer that you actually have the money available. You are not required to release any milestone payments until the work for the milestone is completed. Much like escrow, this protects both you and the freelancer.

Feedback. You are encouraged to leave feedback after the work is completed, and the freelancer will do the same for you. Bad feedback is not helpful for either of you, so there is incentive to do good work on the part of the freelancer and incentive for you to pay on time and provide clear requirements as the hiring party.

Communications. Marketplaces have private messaging capabilities. Any time you want your message to a freelancer to be kept as a matter of record, send a private message. If you ever get into a dispute, the marketplace powers can review your message logs. However, as a practical matter, it is easier to communicate via your platform of choice, be it email, Facebook, Skype, or by phone.

Measure, Measure, Measure

Every business owner knows that improvement starts with measurement. The websites I check up on every day are much more likely to get my care and attention than those I never look at. When I monitor sales and traffic, I can spot opportunities to capitalize on certain customers or certain traffic sources. When I look at my reports regularly, I can assess the effectiveness of changes I made to the website and then repeat the techniques that were successful. While many aspects of a website can be measured and improved, it always pays to focus on traffic and conversions first.

Traffic

Visitors to your site are consumers of your content. They are leads, and hopefully, many of them are paying customers. Get intimate with your customers. You want to know who they are, where they live, what language they speak, and what they are looking at. You want to know how they made their way to your website, where they came from, and whether they have visited before. But probably the most important variable to understand is *why they came*.

"Many of life's failures are people who did not realize how close they were to success when they gave up."
–Thomas Edison

The visitor's *why* is critical because if you understand his motive, you can give him much more of what he is looking for. Did he come to be entertained? Was it because of curiosity or anger? Was he looking for general education or highly specific information? Did he want to buy something, or was he just browsing or collecting information for a future purchase?

I have writers who publish about twenty news articles for me every day. We all have access to detailed analytics information that tells us in real time what visitors are reading, how long they spend on the page, and whether they are hanging around to read more articles or hit the back button to browse elsewhere. We watch that information like a hawk. If readers are interested in the newest Nokia phone on Thursday morning, you better believe we are going to be publishing more articles about that phone until something else is trending higher.

It is important to capitalize on things that are working. If you are seeing good traffic coming from humorous Facebook posts, then that becomes a prime area for experimentation. You would naturally try to create more of the same kind of posts. If that isn't producing a bang for the buck, then identify the most effective posts and pay Facebook the $6 or $7 fee to "promote" a post. If Facebook seems to be a good overall source of traffic, depending on what your revenue model is, consider purchasing highly targeted Facebook ads. Hire a freelancer who specializes in Facebook and social network promotion. The point is to build on your winning traffic sources—whatever they may be. As you experiment, you will identify new sources and tune existing ones.

Google Analytics is a free system for analyzing hundreds of metrics about your website. Diagram 1 is an overview of the kinds of information available. It shows how many people are online, the pages they are browsing, where they are located, what devices they are using, where they came from, and in some cases, the search phrase they used to find the website. This is a real-time overview, and there is a great deal more detail available for each section of the dashboard.

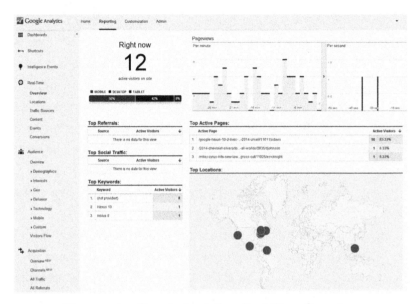

Diagram 1 – Google Analytics, Real-Time Overview

Google Analytics provides traffic source data to help you understand how your visitors are finding your website. In Diagram 2, not surprisingly, about 47% of the traffic is coming from Google Search; 21% is direct, meaning the visitor typed in the name of the URL, had it bookmarked, or came from an unknown source; 9% was from Google News; and smaller percentages came from Zergnet, Bing, and other sources. The website received 69,999 visitors over a period of thirty days. Less than 8% were returning visitors.

Source / Medium ?	Acquisition	
	Visits ? ↓	
	69,999 % of Total: 100.00% (69,999)	
1. google / organic	**32,882** (46.97%)	
2. (direct) / (none)	**14,444** (20.63%)	
3. news.google.com / referral	**6,364** (9.09%)	
4. zergnet.com / referral	**5,490** (7.84%)	
5. bing / organic	**3,479** (4.97%)	
6. stumbleupon.com / referral	**1,125** (1.61%)	
7. google.de / referral	**730** (1.04%)	
8. google.fr / referral	**619** (0.88%)	
9. yahoo / organic	**556** (0.79%)	
10. m.facebook.com / referral	**363** (0.52%)	

Diagram 2 – Google Analytics Acquisition, All Traffic

An important part of your analysis involves looking at the specific pages that are viewed by your visitors. In Diagram 3 we see that the top article attracted 4.5% of the traffic during the thirty-day period. Readers spent just under three minutes reading the article, but only 11% remained on the website to read another article.

Page	Pageviews 95,360 % of Total: 100.00% (95,360)	Unique Pageviews 85,139 % of Total: 100.00% (85,139)	Avg. Time on Page 00:02:15 Site Avg: 00:02:15 (0.00%)	Entrances 78,270 % of Total: 100.00% (78,270)	Bounce Rate 86.38% Site Avg: 86.38% (0.00%)
1. first-look-at-the-htc-one-plus-aka-htc-m8-aka-one-2/11223/djohnson	5,738 (6.02%)	5,149 (6.05%)	00:02:43	5,140 (6.57%)	86.56%
2. /2014-macbook-air-tipped-for-igzo-retina-panel-macbook-pro-to-get-24-hour-battery/10650/thar per	4,221 (4.43%)	3,954 (4.64%)	00:02:54	3,945 (5.04%)	89.66%
3. /google-nexus-10-2-lives-on-tipped-for-mwc-2014-umeli/11011/edans	3,690 (3.87%)	3,357 (3.94%)	00:03:16	3,352 (4.28%)	88.01%
4. /kanye-accuses-press-of-racism-in-latest-rant/10873/emmcknight	2,707 (2.84%)	2,453 (2.88%)	00:03:12	2,446 (3.13%)	85.65%
5. /microsoft-surface-3-to-feature-64-bit-tegra-k1-cpu-surface-mini-could-launch-april/10139/djohn son	2,400 (2.52%)	2,188 (2.57%)	00:02:49	2,179 (2.78%)	87.10%
6. /faking-it-miley-cyrus-admits-her-luscious-locks-were-never-hers/3631/mhoster	1,768 (1.85%)	1,445 (1.70%)	00:01:12	1,401 (1.79%)	81.94%
7. /new-google-nexus-6-concept-mates-lg-g-flex-with-nokia-lumia/9746/djohnson	1,598 (1.68%)	1,446 (1.70%)	00:01:09	1,430 (1.83%)	90.91%

Diagram 3 – Google Analytics Behavior, Site Content

Conversions

Ultimately, you want your customers to take some action that will generate sales. This is a critical area for website success; unfortunately, most website owners neglect or ignore it—to their detriment. The high-level process for increasing conversions is finding out the current baseline (the percentage of customers who make a purchase) and then making changes one at a time, testing them against each other and choosing the one that yields the higher conversion rate. As needed, repeat the process.

Tip: To increase conversions, always start at the top.

The top is the first thing potential customers see that invites them to your website. If your site gets traffic from direct emails, the first thing they see is the *subject* of the email. If you get customers from advertising, the first thing they see is the *headline* in the ad copy. If they come from search engines, the first thing they see is the *title* of the webpage. The first thing they see at the top of your sales funnel determines whether they will enter the funnel; they will either choose to click in or to bypass it completely. It not only affects whether they will open the email or click through to the website, but it also inclines them toward or drives them away from making an eventual purchase.

So what is a good title? If you are providing information, help, or advice, the best titles are those that clearly state what the article will deliver (e.g., "How to Change the Headlight in a 2005 Honda Civic"). A user who wants a quick, specific answer to their question is much more likely to click on a straightforward title that promises a solution. Readers in a predicament are less impressed with attempts at cleverness (e.g., "Shining Light on Honda Maintenance Projects").

Email subject lines should be built to entice the reader to open the email. Curiosity, controversy, and compelling benefits are a few of the many strategies employed in subject lines. For example, who could help but be curious at the following title: "One Beverage You Should Never Drink on Saturday"? Try to think like your potential reader; make the "top" irresistible.

After you have tested the most common top-level exposure of your website, tweak it to improve the entry rate. Then, you are ready to move to the next thing the customer sees. For email marketing, that would be the content of the email itself. More specifically, pay attention to the very first line of your email. That first line needs to be good enough to get the recipient to read the second line. The second line's only purpose is to get the reader to continue to the third line and so on. Eventually, you want the reader to click on the link in the email.

The same process applies to people who see your site in Google search results. The title is critical, and the text underneath the title, called the meta description, is the second most important thing. Then, if you have earned a reader's click, the next thing he will see is your webpage, which may or may not be your homepage, depending on what they were searching for.

"It is not enough that we do our best; sometimes we must do what is required."

—**Winston Churchill**

The top-down method applies to the analysis of your webpage's ability to convert as well. The first thing a reader should see on the webpage is your main headline. You need to have one, and it needs to be big and very descriptive. When the visitor arrives at your site, he has two subconscious questions: Where am I? Is this a useful place for me to be?

Those questions should be answered immediately, attractively, and unambiguously by the headline and sub-title of your page—or sometimes the title of your article. Clever logos, pretty pictures, and catchy phrases, while creative, probably do not answer the questions in the mind of the visitor and may even cause him to quickly surf away. Conversely, clear communication of what your site does and what is to be gained by hanging around will keep the lion's share of the visitors.

Hanging around is the middle game of the conversion sales process. Once the reader has entered your lair, the goal is to keep him on the website, going from page to page. When your content answers his questions and objectives, it builds his trust and convinces him that he has a need. He will feel a call to action to meet that need.

If you want customers to hang around, don't put Exit doors all over the place. Instead, capitalize on natural curiosity. Don't put too much content on a single page. Instead, make it easy for them to answer their most important questions quickly. Customers want to know prices; they want to know about support; they want to know how easy or difficult things are; they want to see demos and pictures; they want to know who else has bought the product and what happened; and they want to know exactly what they are going to get. Make all of these things easy to find with clear menus and simple language.

If your site has landing pages to sell single products, the top-down method is key. The headline is most important, followed by the sub-headline, followed by the first sentence, and so on down the page. Each phrase should encourage the reader to read the next phrase and ultimately to hear the call to action.

Informational or content sites also have the goal of keeping the visitor on the site. Some ad contracts are per page view, meaning the more pages opened by a visitor the more you earn. If you are paid per click on an ad, you want people to view as many pages as possible too. The more pages they visit, the more ads they will be exposed to and the greater the chances that something in an ad will be attractive enough to cause them to click.

Financial Tracking

Marketing is more important than financial record keeping (in my little entrepreneurial mind), but you can never afford to be drunk and disorderly when it comes to the money. At the very least, you want to record every expenditure made in support of the website and maintain a profit and loss statement by month. I often keep a simple spreadsheet that has a tab for the P&L, one for expenses, and a third one for revenue. Depending on the complexity of the site, you may need to have a bigger spreadsheet, use bookkeeping software, or even hire an accountant. I have the distinct pleasure of being married to a former CPA who keeps me out of trouble but still makes me do all my own bookkeeping.

"It's not how much money you make, but how much money you keep, how hard it works for you, and how many generations you keep it for."

–Robert Kiyosaki

While I monitor sales and traffic daily, taking a look at the larger financial picture once a month keeps me focused on growing the bottom line and helps prevent expenses from getting out of line. Diagram 4 is a sample structure for a profit and loss statement (income statement) that you should create and update monthly.

The top section will track your revenue sources, and the bottom section will track your expenses by category. You may choose to track some key metrics by month so that you can see financial performance alongside the metrics that are important for the website. I usually fill in all the months of the year with a budget and then overlay the budget numbers with the actuals and update the budget numbers for the future months.

Diagram 4 – Sample Profit and Loss Statement.
Numbers in gray are estimates.

	Jan	Feb	Mar	Apr	May	Jun
Revenue						
Adsenese	$425	$437	$400	$400	$400	$400
Infolinks	$37	$34	$35	$35	$35	$35
eBooks	$28	$54	$28	$28	$28	$28
Total Revenue	$490	$525	$463	$463	$463	$463
Expenses						
Webhosting	$12	$12	$12	$12	$12	$12
Writers	$120	$90	$100	$100	$100	$100
Advertising	$25	$25	$25	$25	$25	$25
Paypal	$0	$0	$10	$10	$10	$10

Affiliate Commissions	$0	$12	$10	$10	$10	$10
Total Expenses	$157	$139	$157	$157	$157	$157
NET INCOME	$333	$376	$306	$306	$306	$306
Key Metrics						
Number of Sales	2	4	2	2	2	2
Pageviews	5,645	5,733	5,500	5,500	5,700	5,700
Articles Written	15	12	14	14	14	14
Promo Emails	4	6	5	5	5	5

I have evaluated hundreds of websites that did not even have a simple P&L. If you don't have a P&L, you won't know how much the site is earning. You won't know which expenses need managing. You won't be able to fill out a Schedule C on your U.S. federal income tax form accurately. When you test new strategies, like content writing or additional advertising, you won't know whether it was profitable or not. You won't know how much the site generated over the past year or how much it's going to make over the next full year. You will have less credibility if you ever decide to sell the website. And, most importantly, you will miss the strategic opportunity to step back and assess the website as a whole each month.

Budget: a mathematical confirmation of your suspicions.

–A.A. Latimer

This might sound kind of dweebish, but I actually love month end. The first day of the month is my opportunity to make a final calculation of what happened during the previous month, see where I stand across all my websites, and formulate or tweak my plan of action going forward. I take my wife out for dinner, and I give her the news—good or bad. She patiently listens to my scheming ideas for the next period. This is when I decide to hire an extra writer, go buy another app-design website, start an email-marketing campaign, change ad networks, or write a book!

Whether you have one or many websites, little or big, track the financials.

13. A Word About the Mobile World

Smart phone and tablet usage has grown considerably, and websites need to take this trend into consideration. Most of my sites receive between 25% and 45% of their traffic from mobile devices. It varies by the type of website and even varies by page within websites, depending on the kind of information on the page. Tech articles on my news sites get a higher percentage of mobile traffic than political articles. No matter the subject area, it is certain that the percentage of mobile traffic will continue to increase, so it is an important topic for both website buyers and website owners.

Website buyers need to know if the site is "mobile responsive." Mobile responsive sites adjust their layout when viewed on a device with a smaller screen. If the site is not mobile responsive, what will it cost to make it so? What percentage of visitors is coming from mobile devices and is the percentage of revenue from those visitors consistent with the percentage of traffic they represent? If not, is that reasonable or not reasonable? Are responsive ad units being used so that the best performing ad sizes are displayed on different screen sizes? If not, that could be a revenue improvement opportunity.

Website owners should also be concerned with optimizing their sites for mobile users. In addition to making the site mobile responsive or creating an entirely different site for mobile users, the website owner needs to consider whether the mobile user has different needs than the desktop user. Should there be fewer or smaller images? Should there be less text? Should there be a different set of products? Are the tools on the website appropriate? Should the website be complimented with an app that takes advantage of knowing the user's location?

A guide on app investing could fill another book. At this writing, apps are changing hands, but not nearly as many are being bought and sold as websites. Although there are millions of apps in the Google and Apple app stores, their numbers do not approach the nearly 1 billion active websites. When compared to websites, apps are significantly overpriced relative to their current earnings. Most apps are sold based on their "potential earnings," which are suspect. Free apps far outnumber purchased apps. There are successful monetization methods for free apps, but free apps need to have a large install base to pay off.

I expect to see a merger of the kind of tools and functions offered by current apps and the easy accessibility of websites in the future. An "App as a Service" model similar to the "Software as a Service" model will emerge. Apps have to be independently downloaded. Websites can all be accessed from a single browser. The new model will provide app functionality delivered through a generic, browser-like service. You read it here first.

As an example of how unpredictable the ROI with apps is, consider my friend Joel Comm. He created the iFart app that sold over 800,000 copies at $0.99 each. After that success, his organization created and heavily promoted a dozen other apps that earned virtually nothing.

Apps are not going away and cannot be ignored. But making a predictable income from apps that aren't connected to a broader business is difficult and uncertain.

14. Do You Need a Business to Own a Website? No, but...

For small website businesses, the question of whether to officially register a business or not is primarily about risk. A corporation or simple LLC protects your personal assets, to some degree, from a legal judgment against you. Disclaimer: I'm not a lawyer. This is not legal advice. I'm an entrepreneur. These are practical things to consider.

Bigger websites, with more diverse customers, multiple revenue sources, more traffic, more contracted relationships, and more employees or sub-contractors, have more contractual risk. So if you have or plan to buy a complex website, then _you should bite the bullet and register a business_. It is not too difficult or expensive in most parts of the world, and you will sleep better at night. I was able to do it online in my home state for $80 in about twenty-five minutes. Our state requires I file a report every two years, and it takes less than ten minutes to fill out the online form. Filing taxes may or may not be time consuming, depending on the nature of the revenue sources and whether you have employees or not.

LLCs and corporations protect the personal assets of individuals by preventing an LLC member's personal assets from being seized by creditors. The LLC owner is thus protected if the LLC fails to deliver on contracts. There is also some legal protection if an LLC makes a mistake that causes loss or harm. If the owner performs an illegal activity, he is not protected by the LLC. If the LLC fails to operate in a manner that is fully separate from the owner's personal life, the courts may find that the LLC is not really distinct from the owner and may not protect the owner.

Unfortunately for website businesses, LLCs don't protect individuals against torts. Intellectual property infringement is considered a tort, and websites are prone toward IP infringement. Be vigilant in your watch over the site's content; copyright, trademark, and patent violations can and do happen.

Examples of IP infringement violations include the following:

- The use of images without permission
- Misuse of trademarks, like logos or brand names
- Use of snippets of software that are not freeware
- Plagiarism

Some other situations where the LLC might not protect the owner are, as follows:

- Membership sites where customers have not been clearly notified about their right to cancel and the method for doing so. See the Restore Online Shoppers' Confidence Act (ROSCA).
- The marketing of business opportunities, such as the supply of outlets, accounts, and customers. See the FTC video on

this topic: http://www.business.ftc.gov/multimedia/videos/
business-opportunity-rule
- Faked or misleading testimonials

Small or big, websites can be risky if they participate in activities that
are illegal, like violating copyright laws or Federal Trade Commission
laws. Although LLCs do not provide personal asset protection in all
situations, they cover enough scenarios that you should view them as
very low-cost insurance. You should consider buying business insurance
and personal liability insurance for a much more comprehensive risk
avoidance strategy.

15. When to Sell and How to Do It

This book is not about flipping sites per se, but many people love the thrill of the hunt and the even bigger thrill of the sale. Personally, I always hang onto sites that have steady financial earnings and are not too difficult to operate. As the workload grows, I delegate, outsource, or partner with other people to keep my time free to work on other projects. However, there are a lot of good reasons to sell, and I have sold in these and other situations:

- The potential sales value of the website was high, and I knew that I could create a new site in the same niche and quickly replace earnings from the site that was being sold.
- The website had higher-than-expected customer support requirements, and I felt like my time could be spent on more profitable and enjoyable activities.

- The website was very dependent on traffic from Google. Though it was performing well, I had a sense that if Google changed its search algorithm again, the tide might turn. It seemed better to sell the site for ten months' earnings than keep it and risk a traffic hit in the next ten months that would dramatically lower the value of the site.
- I had unwittingly acquired some sites that were legal to operate but pushed the limits of my own personal ethics.
- The website had lost most of its value, and I had no clue how to turn it around. I sold to avoid a total loss.

Website flipping is often compared to real estate flipping. However, beyond the principle of "buy low, sell high," the two have little in common. After a house is purchased and remodeled, it needs to be sold, or it becomes a liability. It is either tying up cash that could be used elsewhere, or it carries ongoing interest and tax expense. After a website is purchased and improved, it is a profitable asset, not a liability. So the rationale for selling a website is fundamentally different than the rationale for selling a house that has been intentionally purchased and remodeled for resale.

The business model of the website flipper is to look for hidden or potential value in websites and buy in at a good price point. The flipper then harvests low-hanging fruit by making relatively simple changes to the website that increase its earnings and overall value. The flipper then sells the website because its overall earning potential has improved, so he can get a much higher price. This strategy works well because the flipper has learned some specific techniques to improve website performance quickly, and those techniques are successful a high percentage of the time. The flipper may not know anything at all about how to take the website to the next higher level or may have no interest in doing so.

Simply put, the flipper spends his time doing three things: buying, improving, and selling.

By contrast, the website investor also does some buying, improving, and selling, but because those activities are not passive, they don't meet one of his main goals, which is to develop passive income streams to preserve his time for more preferable pursuits. I don't want to be dependent on the margin of the next sale for this month's income. As you browse through some of my reasons for selling, you will see a combination of risk aversion, financial prudence, time protection, and simple preference.

Getting the Best Price and Developing Relationships

This section is titled after the two primary goals of the website sales process. The first is to get a good price. The second is to develop a following of buyers and colleagues in the website business to help you down the road. You'll find techniques for achieving both of those things as we look at the details of the sales process.

Preparation

If you operate the website the way you should, tracking the money in a Profit and Loss statement, using Analytics tools to stay on top of traffic and conversions, and keeping records of sales transactions—even if they are in PayPal or your bank account—then you have the data that you will need for your sales listing. The more source documents you can provide as proof of the performance of the website, the better. I collect the following kinds of documents to be used as attachments to my sales listing:

- Proof of revenue, including advertising earnings, affiliate sales transaction logs, PayPal payment entries, screenshots of

checks from Amazon.com, shopping cart transaction logs, and commission payment statements
- Profit and loss statement
- Screenshots of particular events, like high keyword ranking on Google, products featured in magazines or other websites, articles linked to by famous people or websites, analytics showing traffic spikes
- Screen capture video showing proof of revenue by logging into accounts
- Video highlighting the features of the website or business
- Historical sales reports
- Historical traffic reports

Detailed documentation increases buyer confidence and usually decreases the number of questions asked. The exception is when your data raises questions instead of answering them. You should deal with these questions and objections directly in your sales listing.

The caveat in supplying detailed information to prospective buyers is that the information may divulge secrets that could create competition for the buyer of the website and cause harm to you if the sale falls through. You can address this risk by a combination of the following techniques:

- not revealing crucial, secret strategies until the website is sold
- requiring potential buyers to sign a non-disclosure agreement prior to having access to the source documentation
- making certain information known only to buyers you have vetted and at your own discretion (Many website owners browse sales listings for no other reason than to harvest ideas for improving their own websites. Keep that strategy in mind for your website too.)

The Sales Listing

The sales listing, or prospectus, is where you make your pitch to convince the buyer that this is the website for him. The adage that people buy from those they know, like, and trust is true for websites as well. So you let potential buyers know you by telling them your real name and email address and presenting a complete profile, with links to Facebook, LinkedIn, and your personal website.

You help them like you by writing the listing in an unpretentious and appealing way. You respond thoroughly to all their questions, answering in a gentle and profession manner. And you develop trust by being very honest, responsive, thorough, and knowledgeable about your website.

The vast majority of sales listings are terrible. They are not created by people who are naturally good marketers. This fault could give you a considerable advantage. If you invest a little bit of time, you can easily create a listing that is in the top 10% and can probably get to the top 5%. That feat alone won't guarantee you a high price because, ultimately, the website's intrinsic value will dictate the bounds of the pricing, but it will guarantee more visibility to your listing and a much more serious look from people who are qualified buyers.

Be sure to check out "Effective Sales Pitch Components" under Resources at the end of the book.

The Title

The top-down approach to optimization works with website sales listings too, and the "top" in this case is the title of the listing. The title needs to have two or more of the following components:

- Site focus or category: "eCommerce Site;" "Jokes Site;" "Pregnancy Resource"
- Urgency: "Three-Day Auction;" "Quick Sale;" "Motivated Seller"
- Unique feature or attribute: "Award Winning;" "Patented;" "Featured on Oprah"
- Compelling statistic: "$500 Passive Per Month;" "1 Million Visitors Last Year;" "$10,000 in Sales;" "50,000 Downloads"

Keep in mind that the title is the only thing in your listing that most people will see. They will see it as they scroll through marketplace listings. They may see it in Google search results. They may see it in emails if they get notifications from brokers or the marketplace. A weak title will attract no clicks.

The Summary

Begin the listing with a summary of what the website is all about. Buyers want to know quickly what kind of website it is, why people visit it, and what it does. As part of the summary paragraph, you can also state some of the key statistics, like monthly earnings, traffic, or number of sales—as long as it is significant and casts the site in a good light. If the site has no sales, don't mention that in the summary paragraph.

Hype doesn't work in website sales listings. Truth and personality do work. If the site was your labor of love, say so and demonstrate passion in the way you describe its features and your nurture of it. If you bought it based on its brand potential, traffic characteristics, fantastic product line, or beautiful design, say that too. If the site has any external notoriety at all, that fact should be mentioned. Cite links from authority websites or references to the site by television networks and newspapers.

Details

Following the summary, provide more details about the way the website operates. Explain who the visitors are, where they come from, what you want them to do on the page, how you earn money by their actions, and what the owner's role is. You'll say more about how to operate the site further down. You may want to discuss the history of the site, the thinking behind it, and detail some of the bright spots. If there are freelancers or employees associated with the site, explain what they do and how much time it takes. Discuss the niche, the competition, the content sources, and the products.

Revenue and Expenses

List all of the revenue sources, and provide monthly totals for each source. These may be included in a P&L attached to the listing or in other documents, but it is good to provide a summary in the listing description because buyers will browse down through the listing first and may never open the attachments. Do the same thing for expenses by category.

Provide net income totals by month, and make sure they tie correctly to revenue and expenses. Also make sure that the details in the attached documents and spreadsheets agree with the numbers you have placed in the listing.

Traffic

Provide some summary figures for traffic by month. Page views are better than visitors or unique visitors simply because the page-view numbers will be higher. If it is relevant to your website, also explain the demographics of the traffic, like country of origin, whether it is paid or free traffic, and where it comes from. If the stats are favorable, you may also want to put number of pages per visit, percentage of returning visitors, or other flattering statistics.

Why You Are Selling

Because one of the biggest fears in the buyer's mind is that you are selling because the site has a big, undisclosed problem, you want to dispel that fear very clearly in the listing. Write the real reason you are selling, as uncomfortable as that may feel. You will earn tons of trust by being honest here because readers will be able to sense that you are speaking the truth. If the reason is that you need the money for a different project, then tell them what that project is. If another website is taking up all your time, then give them a link to that website. The more detail you provide, the more genuine your reason for selling is going to sound.

If the reason is something that sounds very negative, like the presence of new competitors that will drive sales down or a Google algorithm change that has dropped traffic levels or tons of customer support that you don't like to do, then you still need to be honest, but it is wise to provide a counterbalance. For example, you might write, "A new competitor opened a website two months ago, and I've seen a drop-off in sales since then. Our product is definitely better, but the website needs to be updated to reflect the differences, and I don't have the energy for that right now." If you believe the situation is hopeless and you are truly selling a lemon, then you have a moral obligation to consider not selling at all, or, at the least, you should be succinct and clear about what the challenge is and leave it to the buyers to decide. I feel much better when a site doesn't sell than when a buyer pays a price that is far more than the site is worth.

Growth Potential

Savvy buyers don't pay a lot of heed to seller claims about a website's potential. However, if the seller is successful in gaining trust via the other suggestions in this chapter, his remarks about the potential of the website will carry some weight. Buyers also read the section on potential to help them better understand how the business model of the website works and where the potential growth areas are. The buyer may already have preconceived ideas about how he can improve the website, and if you mention a few ideas he was already thinking of, it can increase his resolve to purchase the site.

In this area, you are going to focus on the same areas I have been harping on throughout the book: increasing conversions; increasing traffic; and increasing sales, via things like price adjustment, new content ideas, or new market channels. The important thing is not to list a bunch of generic stuff (like I just did). Rather, list very specific ideas: publish five additional articles about Topic A, or send emails three times a week instead of once per week. And then include the why: because the current articles about Topic A convert twice as well as those about Topic B, or because our sales were 45% higher when we were sending three emails per week than they were after we cut back to one per week.

What Is Required to Operate the Website?

Here you are answering two more buyer questions that are usually high priority. The first is, "How much effort does it take to operate this website and continue to earn the current level of profit?" And the second question is often, "Do I have the skills to run this website?" You will want to take these questions seriously and answer them clearly with details to support your claims. Here is an example of a sufficient response:

> *This website requires two hours of support per week, on average. We receive about four helpdesk tickets per week, and it takes anywhere from five minutes to twenty minutes to answer each of them. Most of them are related to password resets or something that is already on our FAQ page. We also receive about ten emails a week from our Contact Us page—some of which are spam and others are*

requests for guest posts. You will also want to check the Adsense and Analytics results at least once a week and make a couple of Facebook posts to keep the fan page active.

You also need to address the second question and explain what knowledge is necessary to operate the site. Always describe how the buyer can get up to speed if he doesn't already have the skills or know-how.

About You

I like to include a section about myself that is sometimes titled, "Who You Are Buying From." This section serves one purpose: to develop trust. You just write the truth about who you are, whether you are a retired school teacher, work-at-home mom, part-time website junkie, website investor, website flipper, or student. I sometimes mention my family, the fact that I make a living on the Internet full time, that I lived in Central Asia for seven years doing humanitarian work, or that I was a former senior manager at IBM—whatever revelations seem comfortable.

Link to your profile, especially if you have a track record selling websites and have good feedback. If you plan to sell more websites, include the link that lets buyers follow you and get notifications any time you offer a new site for sale. If you plan to make yourself available to the buyer after the sale, you might want to explain that buying the website gives the buyer access to you, your knowledge, and your contacts in the industry. This is a compelling bonus! I have had many people bid on an auction and lose, only to have them approach me for coaching, training resources, or consulting services to help them build or improve their own websites.

This section may be near the top just after the summary, or it can be farther down in the listing.

Frequently Asked Questions

Include answers to questions and rebuttals to potential objections in a FAQ section. Will the current writer continue writing for the site? How much post-sale support will you provide? Can you continue to host the site? How much do you pay your freelancer? How many Tweets do you send out per week? Will you provide the names and contact info of the suppliers? Have you done backlink building or any other SEO? And on and on. The more details you write, the more comfortable your buyers will feel.

The Auction Process

If you only accept payment via escrow, you should say that here. Who pays the listing fees and the escrow fees? State the length of the inspection period. Will you approve new bidders or only those with a documented track record?

Listing Your Site for Sale on Flippa

This section will explain the specific options you have for listing your site for sale on Flippa, along with recommendations for those options. Other marketplaces may have some of these same options or others that Flippa doesn't have, but the principles will apply just about anywhere that you might list your site for sale.

Clicking on SELL in Flippa will initiate a series of forms prompting you for details about your website. The first decision point is whether to list your website under Flippa's exclusive brokerage service called Deal Flow. Deal Flow is for sites valued at greater than $10,000. Deal Flow auctions are advertised to a group of pre-qualified buyers. Flippa will look at your site and do some pre-validation prior to presenting the listing to its buyer list. The listing fee is free. There is a 10% success fee paid by the seller and a $1,000 finder's fee paid by the buyer at the time of this writing. The benefit to using this service is that you get more personal attention than a normal listing provides. In addition, buyers and sellers are pre-qualified, so you don't have to spend as much time checking each other out and the listings are not made public, so any proprietary info has a more limited viewing audience. The high-end buyers that participate in Deal Flow also look at normal Flippa listings, so you won't necessarily miss out on their perusal, but you will probably have a better chance at attracting their attention with Deal Flow.

The next important question in the listing process is whether to have Google Analytics information verified by Flippa. I suggest you do this if at all possible. This lends credibility to your listing.

When presented with "The Pitch" form, you will enter your listing's title, called Tagline by Flippa. (See the section entitled "Title" earlier in the chapter; it's important.) Then you enter a description, which is the full listing text that you created in preparation for selling your website. It is good to create it in a document outside of Flippa and then paste it into the Flippa form. Check over the formatting and make use of colors, font size, and formatting to add a little excitement to the pitch. Bigger font sizes and attractive formatting make reading your listing a lot easier for buyers, and that's what you want.

Next comes the "Sale" page with four important fields:

1. Sale type. Here you may select *Auction* if you want the sale to occur like a public auction, eBay style. That is by far the most common option chosen and fosters competition among buyers. The second possibility is to select *Private Sale*. Private sales allow you to receive sealed bids from buyers who are unaware of each other's bids or the current highest bid. You as the seller simply receive bids and decide whether you want to accept one of them. There is a private message communication vehicle for both sale types and a public commenting system for the auction sale type.

2. Length of auction. You may choose an auction length between three and thirty days inclusive, or a private sale length of up to 180 days. Longer auctions are likely to be seen by more potential buyers. Website sales of varying auction lengths have been studied, and ten-day auctions seem to produce higher prices on average. My opinion is that very short auctions are not seen by many buyers, so there is less competition. Thirty-day auctions, on the other hand, are so long that people tend to forget about them. There may be an initial interest in the listing, but because bidding activity doesn't happen until the end, many buyers simply never return to the auction to see what happens or participate in the bidding. I actually prefer shorter auctions in the five- to seven-day range because when I decide to sell, I want to get it done. I also invest a lot of time during an auction answering questions and providing instant support. Maintaining that level of attention for an entire month—or even ten days—requires a lot of effort.

3. Starting bid. This is the lowest starting bid a buyer may make. Flippa recommends that it be low enough to encourage early bids but high enough to be indicative of what your reserve price is.

4. Reserve. The reserve price is the lowest amount that you would be willing to accept for your site. Buyers won't know what your reserve price is until a bid has reached the reserve price.

Flippa next presents several options for promoting your listing. "Premium" listings attract eleven times more views and three times the bids, according to Flippa. This claim is consistent with my experience; however, I only recommend this option for websites with a value of $5,000+. There are other promotional options that will make your listing appear on the homepage, bold the title, or add screenshots.

I don't typically take advantage of these other upgrades, with one exception. With 48 hours to go in the auction it is sometimes useful to pay for the option to have your listing appear on the homepage if you don't feel like you have attracted enough serious bidders.

You may also choose to add a non-disclosure agreement to the listing. Prior to bidding and prior to getting access to your URL name and detailed attachments, prospective buyers will be required to sign an NDA. This can be Flippa's standard NDA or your own. The value of this $100 upgrade is not only protection of the website's proprietary information, but also a higher level of perceived value. However, it limits the number of people that will seriously investigate your listing. This might be okay if you are selling a high-value site or one that really does have information you can't afford to get into the hands of the general public.

After making the listing fee payment to Flippa, you will be able to upload attachments to the listing. We discussed the various kinds of documents that you should attach earlier in the chapter, but the key ones are traffic and revenue proof and your P&L. If you have Adsense revenue, use the option to verify that revenue. This is another big confidence builder for your auction. Update the payment method to be escrow only. Then, kick off the auction!

The Auction

After the auction has begun, Flippa will start keeping track of the number of views your auction receives. Brand new auctions are published on Flippa's home page, so you tend to get more traffic in the first twelve to eighteen hours of the auction, depending on how many new listings there are. If all is well, you will soon begin to receive bids—especially if the website is in the low-price range and your minimum bid price is set low.

"An investment in knowledge pays the best interest."
—Benjamin Franklin

Your first decisions will be whether to accept bids you receive. Flippa will notify you that a bid has been made but will not say how much the bid is. The principle is that you must accept "bidders," not "bids." Once you have accepted a bidder, all bids for that bidder will automatically be accepted. Do not accept every bidder. Look at each profile to find previous feedback and history on Flippa. If there is anything that leads you to believe he might be a bad apple, don't accept him. If you are desperate for bidders, write a private message to attempt to collect more information. There are times when I have changed my mind about a suspicious-seeming bidder after a bit of communication with him. A bidder who is brand new to Flippa and who does not provide you any information about his identity presents another difficult case. I recommend that you write to each, requesting more information, before accepting a bid.

What's the danger in accepting a bid from a con artist? The main risk is that he will bid high, win the auction, not pay you, and force you to start over again. Second auctions rarely do as well as first auctions. (Of course, there are exceptions.) Why do cons do this? Heck if I know. Maybe they are fishing for more information. Maybe they genuinely want to own the site but can't afford it. Don't be so afraid of this possibility that you eliminate a serious buyer. Just be aware and beware.

At the end of the auction, Flippa will provide the name and contact info of the winning buyer. It is good to continue to use the site's private messaging system for at least the preliminary and important communications with the buyer so that if there is a dispute of any kind, Flippa can see the chain of events and have justification to support you. You will also see an Escrow.com button you can use to initiate the escrow transaction. Using Flippa's button gives you a discount off of the normal escrow fees. There is also a sample "Contract of Sale" you can use if you want a contract and don't want to write your own.

That's what you need to know about Flippa from a seller's perspective. There is a lot more detail on the post-sale phase of an auction in the chapter entitled "The Handoff."

Communications

You need to be the consummate professional in all your communications, both public and private, throughout the auction. Answer every question promptly, politely, and thoroughly. When people make critical or antagonistic public comments, respond graciously and thoroughly. Always take the high ground. Consistently respond as if the question is a good question—even if you already answered it in your listing or elsewhere. Do not be arrogant. This is how authority and trust is established. There is often an unspoken question behind the written question, and you get more points by answering both of them.

Written Question	Unspoken Question	Your Answer
Why are the sales numbers in your listing higher than those in your PayPal documentation?	Are you hiding something?	Excellent question. Thanks for pointing that out. The PayPal numbers include refunds, which were 2% of sales last month. The listing number is the gross sales amount. I would be happy to show you more details via Skype if you are interested.

| Have you experimented with different ad placements? | Is this site tapped out, or is there still potential to make some tweaks that will improve revenue? | Great question. I'm using the same ad positioning I use on my other content sites because it seems to yield good click-through rates on ads. The buyer of this site should test different placement options, look at ad performance—with and without the sidebars—and maybe even try additional ad networks. I was using what worked on other sites, but I know from experience that every site is a bit different and will benefit from optimization specific to that site. |

It is best to respond immediately to comments and questions throughout the auction. If you don't have time for that, tell everyone exactly how often you will be checking in and then keep to that promise. Encourage serious buyers to call you and offer to set up times to share your screen with them to show financial and traffic proof and answer questions. You are building relationships through the whole process that will prove helpful in the future—regardless of who buys the site.

It is common to be asked questions about the price you are looking for. They come in different forms, such as the following:, Can you share the reserve price? How much do you expect to get by the end of the auction? What is your price range? Will you close the auction if I give you $2,000 right now? Do you realize your buy-it-now price is way out of line?

The unspoken questions and intent are along these lines: Can I afford this? Should I invest any time researching this website as it might be out of my price range? Is there any possibility I can get a real bargain on this website? Can I convince him to let it go early and at a good price?

Your goals are, as follows:

- To keep buyers interested, keep them watching the listing, keep them asking questions
- To give them hope that they can walk away with the website at a great price
- Not to cap the amount the site will ultimately sell for
- To do all of the above without lying and without sounding like you are lying

You accomplish this by doing the following:

- Telling them that the reserve price is set much lower than the true value of the site (This needs to be true, by the way.)
- Encouraging them to place a bid, even it if is a low one (Getting them to take any action at all keeps them engaged in the game.)
- Sharing information about other potential buyers if and when it helps motivate the buyer you are talking to. For example, if the current buyer seems worried about competing buyers, you can tell him there aren't any or very few (again, provided this is true). If the current buyer is skeptical about the value of the website, then you might want to share how many other buyers are showing high levels of interest and, if appropriate, the kinds of questions they are asking.
- Explaining untapped potential of the website
- Updating the listing with more current sales and traffic statistics throughout the auction
- Not making any price-related commitments early in the auction

Case Study: A Soft Spot for Software

Of the six companies with the biggest cash reserves worldwide, three are software companies: Microsoft, Google, and Oracle. For two more, Apple and Cisco, software is a large component of their product success and profit margins. The last is Pfizer because there is always a drug company in any "top" or "best of" list. The conclusion is clear: there is big money in software. That statement is not a secret.

The secret is that getting into the software business is not that difficult. I started by investigating website clones.

Every popular product gets copied, and that's what software clones are. There are clones of Facebook, eBay, Pinterest, Twitter, Google, and every other website that has made a big splash. Who would want his own eBay, Facebook, or Google? I was surprised that the answer is "a lot of people."

Consider these scenarios. A photographer lay in bed at night, thinking, "What if there was an eBay especially for camera enthusiasts?" He woke up the next morning, did a few searches on the web, and found out that he could buy his very own "eBay-like" website template that could be fully customized to appeal to photographers everywhere. Judy dreams of a website that looks like Pinterest but is filled with pet pictures. She wonders whether the name Peterest.com is taken. Hank creates Hanksbook from a clone script he finds on Hotscripts.com.

I picked up my most recent clone website for 7x net earnings. Included in the sale was the clone software itself, which was designed by the seller and created for her by a freelance programmer. There was also the website that sold the software, a demo of the software, a helpdesk system, a licensing system, and all the documentation.

The seller had decided to create the clone herself because three years earlier there was only one other clone available, and it had some major deficiencies. It cost her $1,500 per month to have the initial software created, and after a few short months, she was consistently earning that $1,500 back every month.

She answered pre- and post-sale questions herself. Occasionally, there were bugs in the software or problems she couldn't solve, so she had the freelancer take care of fixing those since she wasn't a programmer. Every year or so, she also had him build in new features to be sold as a new release.

I had three big questions: Were ownership rights of the software clear? Why do people keep buying the software? How much work does it take to run the site? The seller had applied for an official copyright of the software. She had no idea why people continued to buy the software, but the revenue proof was clear. After three years there was still a consistent flow of new customers buying every month. The third answer was the rub. On the one hand, in the sales listing, the seller described the workload as light. She explained that there were only an average of two customer support tickets per week, and they were easy to address. But in private conversation, she admitted that her real reason for selling was because she was tired of customer support and wanted to focus her time on another website that didn't require support.

Although I rather despise being a helpdesk myself, when I looked at the few hours to provide support versus the profit to be had, I decided it was kind of silly not to go for it. Besides, I had some ideas on how to reduce the support requirements.

Sales were strong the first several months and then declined when a competitor released a new product. At the current pace, the site will pay for itself in fourteen months. Customer support, though sometimes trying, occupies very little time. Here's the scorecard for this clone site:

Goal: Low effort or no effort	Result: Low effort / stress
Although the site qualifies for a low-effort rating based on the very few minutes required per week, sometimes the customers are demanding, which increases the stress and causes me to give it a so-so score in this area.	

Goal: Low risk	Result: Some risk
The site is dependent on Google traffic, but because it is competing on relatively rare search terms, this risk is manageable. Also, paid advertising supplements the free traffic flow to further decrease the risk. A potential risk that customers will no longer want the product can be mitigated to some extent by enhancing the product over time.	

Goal: Long life	Result: Unclear
This is difficult to assess. Traffic and sales have declined somewhat. The site this software is cloned from continues to grow.	

Goal: Google resistant	Result: Yes
The site has not reacted to Google algorithm changes, but traffic has dropped off some due to new competition.	

Goal: Short payback period	Result: Acceptable
Payback is on track for fourteen months.	

Goal: High quality service	Result: Good quality
The product is better than the competition in most cases, so it delivers the value it promises. I have found many more bugs than the seller acknowledged. Most customers do not perform the marketing of their websites that is required to be successful with their websites, and I do not currently provide a service to help them do that.	

What To Do Next

For additional services and resources on website investing,
visit **http://HeckYeah.org**

Need help evaluating, buying or selling an online business?
Contact Jeff directly at **Jeff@HeckYeah.org**

About The Author

Jeff Hunt has bought and sold over three hundred income-producing websites. He is a former IBM Project Executive and missionary.

Jeff makes his home in Indianapolis with his wife Becky and children, Mason, Holly, Kelton, and Anna, where they are active in their church and community.

Keep up with Jeff at **HeckYeah.org**.

Acknowledgments

Joel said, "You ought to write a book." And he was right. Thanks for the impetus and encouragement.

It's an honor to be a new member of the Morgan James family. Mucho thanks to David and the whole team.

I'm indebted to Becky, who has put up with my entrepreneurial ADD for years. I'm grateful to Chris, Tim, Wally, John, Ted, Nancy, Deanna, Simon, Ron, Scott, George, and others who read the manuscript and provided invaluable insights. Thank you John for your friendship, partnership and constant encouragement. Teachers are vastly improved by students. My coaching clients and students of "Own the Web" at Website-Investors.com have collectively helped me understand what to emphasize in this book.

I have nothing I haven't received from the Lord. To Him be all glory and praise.

Resources

The Website Buying Process

Set Goals
- Amount you are willing to spend
- Desired niche
- Preferred business model
- Website's minimum earnings
- Website's minimum age
- Website's minimum traffic

Search
- Choose marketplaces and brokerages to target
- Setup automated notifications

Evaluate Top Picks
- Verify revenue
- Verify traffic
- Verify ownership
- Verify expenses
- Assess risk
- Evaluate customers
- Evaluate backlinks
- Evaluate content
- Evaluate competition
- Evaluate seller's reasons for selling
- Evaluate dependencies
- Assess your own knowledge of the nich and business model
- Evaluate future potential

Buy
- Negotiate
- Bid
- Close the deal

Transfer
- Transfer domain
- Transfer Analytics accounts
- Transfer social network accounts
- Transfer affiliate accounts
- Transfer advertising accounts
- Setup web hosting
- Transfer database
- Transfer website files
- Setup email accounts
- Transfer documentations
- Transfer physical assets
- Establish relationships with suppliers, customers

Improve
- New monetization methods
- Profit and revenue improvements
- Traffic improvements

Operate
- Monitor sales
- Monitor traffic
- Monitor expenses
- Monitor customer experience
- Add content
- Track financials

Effective Sales Pitch Components

Title
- Category of site
- Unique features
- Urgency
- Compelling stats

Summary
- Site purpose
- Business model
- Key statistics

Details
- Complete description
- Customers
- Products
- Site content
- History
- Process

Revenue Expenses
- Revenue sources
- Revenue totals
- Key expenses
- Total expenses
- Net profit by month

Growth Potential
- Traffic
- Conversion improvement
- New products
- New content
- Expense reduction

Traffic
- Visitors by month
- Page views by month
- Other pertinent stats like country, mobile, social media sources

Reason for Selling
- Be honest
- Provide assurance there are no significant flaws or risks

Labor Required

- Hours per week
- Who does it
- Suggestions for outsourcing or delegation

About You

- Transparency to build trust

Proof Documents

- Revenue proof
- Verified Adsense if applicable
- Expenses proof
- Traffic documents, verified where possible
- Income Statements
- Promotion proof (Featured on Fox News...)
- Product Photos
- Supplier agreements
- Sales Prospectus
- Website operational instructions, nonproprietary
- Links to Proof videos